RETIREMENT ARMOR

RETIREMENT ARMOR

THE SURVIVAL GUIDE TO SHIELD YOUR WEALTH, SECURE STEADY INCOME, AND STRATEGIZE FOR THE UNEXPECTED

Donald L. Ross, RFC®

BEST SELLER PUBLISHING

Published by Best Seller Publishing®, St. Augustine, FL
Best Seller Publishing® is a registered trademark.
Printed in the United States of America.
ISBN: 978-1-962-59555-1

For more information, please write:
Best Seller Publishing®
1775 US-1 #1070
St. Augustine, FL 32084
or call 1 (626) 765-9750
Visit us online at: www.BestSellerPublishing.org

CONTENTS

FOREWORD

As host of the nationally syndicated Financial Safari Radio Show, my number one objective is to educate the consumer on the advantages and disadvantages of all the financial products and strategies in the monetary world today. It isn't easy to keep track of what's out there and be able to distinguish between an ideal financial fit and a horrific financial recipe for catastrophe. This book is a financial flight plan and will awaken any reader's fiscal self-defense instincts. Don Ross's safety-first philosophy, demonstrated by his "ARMOR UP Your Cash Flow Strategy", will show everyone that he was playing chess when everyone else was playing checkers!

Just as Paul Revere was a true American Patriot with his legendary ride, Don's enchanting narrative spins a cautionary tale of the financial world, and by authenticating it in writing, it is my opinion he will protect countless financial lives! Too many people today are on a disastrous trajectory with respect to their economic plan, and they have no clue. They will wake up when their retirement financial Titanic hits the iceberg of reality, but by then it will be too little, too late. Your retirement planning has got to be done right the first time. You don't get a second chance because if you get to retirement age before you wake up, and you realize you haven't planned properly or haven't planned properly at all, there's nowhere to go. You have written your own financial future in ink with no chance to make corrections.

With eleven chapters bursting with skillful information, Don has accomplished what all authors set out to do when they sit down with a pen and a blank piece of paper; he has created a masterpiece, a "perfect 10"!

My pith hat is off to Don, as he has put in writing many of the goals and desires that we try to accomplish on our weekly show. Job well done, Don!

Peter "Coach Pete" D'Arruda

ACKNOWLEDGEMENTS

Thanks Dad, for teaching me life's most important lessons and Mom for teaching me what grace, love, and compassion means. Thanks to each of my siblings, Nancy, Sue, Jayne, John, and Amy, for the great family memories and that occasional family battle back in the day.

Family Picture 1984

Present Day Family Picture

Thank you to my incredible and loving wife, Joni, and our three amazing children, Lance, Ryan, and Judith. It has been one of life's greatest joys to help guide you and share this journey together. We are truly blessed with a wonderful family and dear friends.

To my colleagues and peers across the country with whom I've had the privilege to collaborate: you are among the many reasons I cherish being an independent retirement advisor. The insights we've exchanged during symposiums, webinars, conference calls, and joint client cases have profoundly enriched this work and inspired much of this book.

To my clients: thank you for granting me the honor of serving you and the privilege of building lasting friendships along the way.

And to the countless others who have touched my life—youth pastors, school friends, Bible study companions, army pals, and even a few unforgettable drill sergeants—your influence has shaped me into the person I am today. Each chapter, each relationship, has left an indelible mark on my journey.

Wishing peace, joy, and love to all of you.

PREFACE

Read this book if...

- You have retired or will retire soon and you're interested in strategies for the future, not the past.
- You realize the big brokerage firms and banks are interested in their own bottom line not yours when you want unbiased advice.
- You realize how important structuring a "RETIREMENT CASH FLOW" plan is.
- You want to protect that security and not go backwards.
- You want to make money in good times and protect it in bad times.
- You are tax conscious and realize it's not what you make, but what you keep.
- You want some of your retirement income guaranteed, consistent, and reliable.
- You realize a change is needed from accumulating (when working) to preservation and protection (at or near retirement).
- You are active, generally happy, and fun to be around.
- You have a feeling a lot of taxes are due on your retirement accounts and need to learn some tax savings strategies.

- You are open minded, enjoy being educated, and realize hope is not a strategy.
- You appreciate the team approach, which provides harmony in your planning and access to all the necessary advisors in one place: experts in investments planning, estate planning, income planning, tax strategies, Medicare and social security planning, banking and even funeral pre-planning.

This book is designed to share some practical ideas for every retirement-minded person to think and act. For writing purposes, "him or he" is gender-neutral. Whether male or female, single, divorced, widowed, gay, straight, black, white, orange, Asian, American, etc., everyone should **ARMOR UP** their retirement savings.

If you are one or all of the above, you will find this book very useful and our advice exceptionally valuable. With many changes due to politics, deficits, Wall Street and bank losses, Americans realize they must protect their retirement savings. Changing Social Security and pensions have become the new "normal", so Americans must have an alternative plan for these changes. In this book you will learn:

- How to create a guaranteed "pension like" retirement paycheck to ARMOR UP your savings...for life!
- Myths aren't dangerous to your retirement income unless you believe and act on them. Which retirement savings, spending, and investments myths are you falling for?
- How to create an abundant life of income, if you are, like many people, without a pension.
- Why certain advisors are not appropriate for retirement planning.
- How to fully uncover fees you are paying and not aware of.
- How to properly invest for retirement and pre-retirement.

- How to minimize taxes in retirement.
- Proven strategies to make sure legal or financial or healthcare mistakes/events do not derail your abundant retirement.
- How to take your retirement savings, enjoy it for your life, and leave a legacy for your heirs.
- Why it is "OK" to graduate from an accumulation advisor/broker to a retirement planning advisor.
- It all boils down to why you must ARMOR UP your retirement. This will ensure The 5 Critical Areas to a successful retirement are in line.

INTRODUCTION

Basic Training 1982

I had the privilege of growing up in Columbus, Ohio, surrounded by five siblings and two loving, attentive parents who shaped my early years with care and encouragement. After graduating from Upper Arlington High School in 1981, I joined the Ohio Army National Guard, where I was trained in field artillery. Thanks to the GI Bill, I pursued higher education at Franklin University and proudly graduated in 1987.

In 1990, I took on a new challenge and enrolled in flight school to become an Army helicopter pilot—an experience that was both thrilling and transformative. I continued my service in the Ohio Army National Guard until retiring on January 1, 2007.

But my commitment to service didn't end there. In 2018, I re-enlisted in the U.S. Army Reserves, serving as a career counselor and achieving the rank of Chief Warrant Officer 4 (CW4). After a fulfilling career, I retired in March 2023 upon reaching the retirement age of 60. It has been both an honor and a privilege to serve as a citizen-soldier.

Throughout my life, values like discipline, honor, duty, and love of country have guided me. This mindset has always driven me to step up and serve when called. That same spirit inspired me to create this book—a **Retirement Survival Guide**—a resource to help others navigate this important phase of life with confidence and preparation.

I hope you enjoy reading it and find it both helpful and inspiring.

Flight School 1990

In the following pages, I share concepts and strategies designed for those approaching or navigating retirement—typically individuals between the ages of fifty and eighty. My goal is to educate and provide insight into the thoughts, concerns, and advice you might want to consider as you plan your retirement journey.

It's important to note that this is not a book of specific recommendations. After all, we may not have met yet, and I don't know your unique situation. When I do offer advice, it's always tailored to the individual, because no two retirement plans are the same.

This book is intended to be thought-provoking—a collection of ideas and observations drawn from years of experience, presented in a concise format. Should we ever sit down together, the conversation will be entirely focused on your personal retirement dreams and goals. My role is to help you create the abundant retirement you deserve.

Think of this as a 30,000-foot view—a broad discussion to help you gain clarity and perspective as you plan for the next chapter of your life.

Veteran's Day 2005, me (far left) and my co-pilot landed a Blackhawk at a local middle school for a Veterans' Day Event

THE MEETING THAT CHANGED MY CAREER

Early in my career, I worked as an agent for IDS Life. While the experience was valuable, I eventually made the decision to become an Independent Advisor, Investment Advisor Representative, and Fiduciary. I left the large investment firm because I believed I could better serve my clients with unbiased advice, free from the limitations of a corporate agenda.

In 1994, I had a meeting that would redefine my professional path. I sat down with a teacher, whom I'll call "Susan," who was preparing to retire from Dublin City Schools. Susan had concerns about her retirement—questions I wasn't yet fully equipped to answer. At the time, my focus was primarily on offering insurance products, and I realized that I lacked the expertise to address the specific challenges she faced as she approached retirement.

That single conversation was a turning point for me. It opened my eyes to how many people were in similar situations and how few advisors were truly prepared to guide them through the complexities of retirement planning. Motivated by this realization, I shifted the focus of my career and committed to specializing in retirement income planning, tax reduction strategies, and estate planning.

Susan had been with her broker for over two decades. While he had been instrumental in helping her during the accumulation phase of her financial journey, he wasn't equipped to guide her through the critical transition to retirement. Susan was looking for safe income strategies tailored to her unique situation—options her current advisor wasn't offering. She wanted peace of mind, clarity, and a plan that reflected her specific needs at this pivotal stage of her life.

When Susan decided to work with me and my team, we were able to offer her a comprehensive approach. As an independent advisor, I could provide her with safe income strategy options, asset protection plans, and long-term growth opportunities. This marked the beginning of a new phase in her financial life—a time focused on preserving and protecting the assets she had worked so hard to accumulate, while also creating the safe income she needed to enjoy her retirement.

I've seen this same scenario play out for many of my clients over the years—especially those coming from "captive" organizations like banks and large brokerage firms. These organizations are often focused on the accumulation stage of wealth building, leaving a critical gap when it comes to retirement income planning. Retirement requires a completely different mindset, one that emphasizes asset preservation, income generation, and peace of mind.

Thanks to Susan, I found my calling in helping individuals navigate this important transition. Her story continues to remind me of the profound impact an advisor can have when they truly understand and address the needs of retirees.

CAPTIVE BROKERS

I'm not saying that banks or brokerages don't care about their clients—they absolutely do. The difference lies in what they can offer. These institutions often sell their own lines of retirement investment products, which means their advisors are "captive" to the firm's offerings.

Think of it this way: if you wanted to buy a reliable, spacious, and reasonably priced minivan, would you go to a Porsche dealership? Of course not. A Porsche dealership is a "captive" seller—they only sell high-end sports cars, which may be great, but they're not what you need. Similarly, captive brokers are limited to their company's products, even if those products may not be the best fit for you.

For example, if you visit your neighborhood bank to purchase a mutual fund, chances are it will be a fund with the bank's name on it. Is that fund the best option for you? Maybe—but maybe not. It's likely an in-house product that the bank's advisors are trained to sell, which might also carry higher commissions.

Throughout this book, I'll share stories of clients who came to us after working with these types of firms. Many of them discovered that their previous advisors focused more on general wealth accumulation rather than the specific needs of retirement planning. At Ross Wealth Advisors, we specialize exclusively in retirement planning because we understand the unique challenges and opportunities retirees face.

Retirement-minded individuals need more than just investment products—they need a comprehensive plan. Our approach addresses every facet of retirement: investment strategies, income planning, legacy planning, tax reduction strategies, and long-term healthcare considerations.

We do things differently. I've met with countless clients who came to us with portfolios that were still structured as if they were in their thirties—heavy on accumulation, light on preservation and income generation. Retirement requires a shift in focus from growing wealth to protecting it, generating income, and ensuring it lasts. That's where we come in.

TWO TYPES OF FINANCIAL ADVISORS

1. **Accumulation Advisors:**
   These advisors focus on helping you build or accumulate wealth during your prime earning years, typically from your twenties through your fifties. During this phase of life, you have the advantage of time, allowing you to take on more risk, pursue big gains, and weather potential losses. The primary goal during this stage is growth.
2. **Preservation and Protection Advisors:**
   As you approach retirement—usually within two to five years—or enter your retirement years, your financial priorities shift. The focus moves from growth to protection, ensuring the assets you've worked so hard to accumulate are preserved and provide a stable income throughout your retirement.

Preservation and Protection Advisors think differently. Our mission is centered on risk minimization and peace of mind. I am proud to be a Preservation and Protection Advisor. My role is to help safeguard your retirement assets, ensuring they remain secure and effective regardless of what's happening in the economy, stock market, or tax landscape.

Our approach is designed to withstand the ups and downs of Main Street, Wall Street, and Washington, D.C., providing you with confidence and security. At Ross Wealth Advisors, we call this **The ARMOR UP Strategy**—a comprehensive plan for preserving and protecting your retirement savings while creating the abundant retirement you deserve.

THE ARMOR UP STRATEGY

Armor is a protective covering designed to prevent harm or injury. But here's the key: armor only works if you put it on. That same principle applies to managing your retirement portfolio—protection comes from preparation.

When I say **"Armor Up,"** I'm talking about actively taking steps to safeguard your assets, income, and future. **ARMOR UP** is more than just a retirement plan—it's like body armor for your financial future, designed to help you withstand the unpredictable swings of the stock market. By focusing on all five critical areas of a successful retirement, it builds a strong foundation so you can face the future with confidence and resilience.

THE 5 CRITICAL AREAS OF RETIREMENT

1. **A**sset Transfer - Estate Plan
2. **R**isk Management - Investment Plan
3. **M**edical - Long Term Health Care Plan
4. **O**utstanding Taxes - Strategic Tax Mitigation Plan
5. **R**etirement Income Plan

Leaving out even one of these key areas could put your retirement at risk. **ARMOR UP** is about replacing uncertainty with understanding and ensuring you have the peace of mind you deserve for an abundant retirement.

You'll hear me reference **ARMOR UP** often because protecting your financial future isn't just my priority—it's my responsibility. Together, we'll build a retirement strategy that stands strong against whatever comes your way.

POTENTIAL DISASTER OR ABUNDANT RETIREMENT?

If you're preparing for retirement or are already retired, you understand the importance of managing a finite pool of money. That money must last not only for the rest of your life but also for your spouse's, if you're married. Without the guidance of an advisor who specializes in **The 5 Critical Areas of Retirement**, you could unknowingly be putting your financial future at risk.

Over my 30 years in the industry, I've met with countless individuals who've watched the value of their retirement savings decline significantly. As we grow older, the margin for error—the "runway" for correcting mistakes—shrinks. That's why I can't emphasize enough the importance of working with an advisor who takes a **holistic approach** to retirement planning, addressing every facet: investments, income, legacy, taxes, and healthcare. This approach can mean the difference between a derailed retirement and one of abundance and peace of mind.

This book is designed to prompt you to think critically about your retirement. My hope is that as you evaluate your current path, you'll recognize the value of seeking a second opinion to ensure you're on track for the secure and fulfilling retirement you deserve.

Consider the idea to ARMOR UP your retirement savings! Yes, it is my abbreviation, but I hope as you read ARMOR UP, you will sense I'm driving home the point to:

- Protect
- Shield
- Preserve
- Avoid harm

with your income, your estate, your taxes, and your money.

THE "BIG FOUR" TOP RETIREMENT FEARS

The top concerns I hear from those facing retirement, or those who are already retired, are:

- Outliving their savings
- Excessive taxes
- Healthcare costs
- Protecting their money

Let's take a quick look at each of these concerns and how each one could impact you.

Outliving your Savings

How do you know how much you can safely spend? Do you have a plan that will take you to 100 years old?

Excessive Taxes

Paying taxes could be the largest cost you will pay in your lifetime and at death. And as I've shared with many, if you don't have a plan, Uncle Sam has a plan for you.

Healthcare costs

This can be the hole in the bottom of the bucket and something that is hard to predict. With healthcare costs continuing to rise what is your best defense?

Protecting your money

Does your retirement plan have a strategy in place for the next significant market drop or correction? If the market were to decline by 20% to 30%, would your savings—and your peace of mind—still be secure? Now is the time to plan accordingly.

You've likely heard the tale that Warren Buffett pays less in taxes than his administrative assistant. Here's what I believe: financially savvy individuals who have accumulated wealth seek expert advice, particularly about tax-saving strategies. Those who act on solid guidance gain the peace of mind that comes with knowing their hard-earned retirement accounts are working efficiently—delivering maximum rewards with the least possible tax burden.

This book is intended purely for educational purposes. Why? Because an educated consumer is an empowered consumer. When you understand the landscape of retirement planning, you're better positioned to make informed decisions that benefit your future.

It's astonishing but true: some people spend more time planning their summer vacation than they do preparing for retirement. Why is that? I believe it comes down to three key reasons:

1. **Procrastination** – Retirement may feel far off or overwhelming, leading many to delay important planning.
2. **Uncertainty** – People often doubt whether the advice they're receiving is tailored to their unique situation.
3. **Fear** – Poor communication or scare tactics from advisors can lead to "investment paralysis," where the fear of making a mistake results in doing nothing at all.

If you recognize yourself in any of these scenarios, perhaps it's time for us to sit down and talk. Together, we can create a customized plan that protects your assets, minimizes taxes, and ensures your retirement is one of abundance and confidence.

WHO IS THE RIGHT RETIREMENT ADVISOR FOR YOU?

An optimal advisor is independent—not tied to a bank, insurance company, mutual fund, or brokerage firm. They are a fiduciary, legally bound to put your best interests first. They are your partner, committed to helping you achieve an abundant retirement, no matter the economy, political landscape, or how long you live.

The purpose of this book is to introduce you to the kind of retirement advisor I am, share my philosophy for preserving and protecting your retirement assets, and explain how you might benefit from our approach.

How do you find out if we're the right fit? It's simple. If we meet, we will review your accounts together and discuss your options. This includes a complimentary, comprehensive analysis of critical components such as pensions, Social Security benefits, and income strategies to ensure your money lasts a lifetime. Armed with the facts, you'll be in control—able to make informed, confident decisions about your future.

Some readers may not feel the need to read any further. If you're ready to explore your specific retirement options now, I encourage you to reach out to me directly at **don@rosswealthadvisors.com**.

For others, who prefer to dive deeper and gather as much information as possible, I encourage you to keep reading. Everyone has their own approach, and this book is designed to provide valuable and transparent education for all styles.

Your retirement goals and dreams matter. I believe everyone deserves the chance to live an abundant retirement. Together, it would be my privilege to help you **ARMOR UP** and secure yours. The bottom line, folks, is that you must **ARMOR UP** your retirement to ensure **The 5 Critical Areas** for a successful retirement are properly aligned.

ASSET TRANSFER - ESTATE PLAN

How To Use Legal Resources To Armor Up Your Estate

The "A" in ARMOR. Asset Transfer - Estate Plan.

Estate planning means preparing for the inevitable: passing away. Let's discuss how to ARMOR UP your estate and avoid common pitfalls.

Take Tom and Carol as an example—a situation more common than you might think.

Tom and Carol had been happily married for 45 years, sharing a loving relationship and a typical will. Tom's will left everything to Carol, and Carol's will left everything to Tom.

When Carol passed away first, Tom arranged a beautiful ceremony for her, attended by their children and grandchildren. A few weeks later, Tom received a visit from the "Casserole Girls," kind neighbors delivering meals to support him in his grief.

Over time, one of these kind-hearted women, Linda, began spending time with Tom. They dated for several months, and eventually, Tom proposed. After a couple of years of enjoying their second chance at love, Tom passed away.

Soon after Tom's passing, Linda was visited by a neighbor named Steve, a widower who came by to check on her. They began sharing coffee every Tuesday morning. One thing led to another, and eventually, Linda and Steve got married.

Now, what's the issue here? The problem lies in what happens to Tom and Carol's estate. With little to no estate planning, their carefully built assets are now controlled by Steve and Linda, even though Steve and Linda had nothing to do with building that estate.

This situation isn't uncommon, and no harm is intended by anyone. It's simply the result of poor or nonexistent estate planning. A scenario like this, which could create havoc, can easily be avoided with a simple estate planning meeting.

It's crucial to consult a trained and experienced estate planning attorney. Our attorney, Bob Hendrix, works directly with our clients here in the office and can provide the necessary services. Rest assured, a complex and costly trust isn't always the answer. Often, a straightforward estate plan is all that's needed.

The key to success is collaboration between your financial advisor and estate planning attorney. This team approach ensures your investments and documents are properly aligned. Without this preparation, you risk losing control of your estate and creating unnecessary stress for your heirs

ARMOR UP means avoiding probate court, minimizing taxes, and passing on as much of your estate as possible to the people you care about—not Uncle Sam. Estate planning is about abundance.

Our goal is for you to enjoy your retirement to the fullest. But when the time comes, after a long and fulfilling life, we want to ensure your estate is executed smoothly, without excessive taxes or probate complications.

For a small investment of time and resources, you can ensure your estate is in order. It's that simple—and that important.

Many people assume that having a will is enough. But estate planning is more than that. While it's not an easy topic to discuss, planning for death is a necessary part of life.

Here are some questions to consider for yourself and your loved ones:

- How can I limit tax consequences for my heirs?
- How can I ensure my estate avoids probate and its impact on my heirs?

- Do I need a trust?
- Do I need a power of attorney?
- Do I need a living will? If I'm in a vegetative state, will my wishes be honored?

Since I am not an attorney, I can only provide basic definitions of these directives. However, I can recommend qualified attorneys we've worked with to guide you through this important process.

FINANCIAL POWER OF ATTORNEY

A Financial Power of Attorney is a document that grants someone the authority to handle your financial matters and make decisions if you are unable to do so.

This can be crucial. Imagine your only savings is an IRA, and you become incapacitated. Now, let's say your wife needs access to funds for your immediate care. She calls the IRA firm and says, "Hi, I need about $20,000 to address some medical expenses."

The representative responds, "Of course, Mrs. Jones. Just bring in the financial power of attorney, and we'll get you a check right away."

But—yikes! She doesn't have one. Is that really the moment you want to discover this critical oversight?.

LIVING WILL

A Living Will, also called an "advance directive," outlines your medical care preferences if you become incapacitated. Remember the Terry Schiavo case in Florida? Her husband stated she wouldn't want to live in a vegetative state, but the state refused to honor that wish, leading to a highly emotional and publicized debate. It was heart-wrenching for everyone involved. To avoid such situations, ensure your attorney—or ours, if you work with us—explains all the details of creating a comprehensive Living Will.

LAST WILL AND TESTAMENT

Most people understand that a will is a written and witnessed document stating who inherits your assets and where they go. Straightforward, right? However, I often hear people say, "It's in my Will that my kids get my IRA when I die." Yikes! Not even close. What many don't realize is that assets like retirement accounts, bank accounts, brokerage accounts, life insurance, or even your home, designated with a beneficiary, payable-on-death (POD), or transfer-on-death (TOD) arrangement, are not directed by your Will. Thankfully! Why? Because, as an attorney once told me, "A Will is an invitation to probate." We'll get into that next.

I usually suggest that a Will is best suited for "other assets," such as the items decorating or furnishing your home.

Beware: If you die without a Will ("intestate"), probate court will take time to determine who is legally entitled to your assets. That process can drag on and cost thousands in legal fees. Why? Because anyone could show up in court claiming a stake in your estate. Plus, since probate is a public process, all your "stuff" becomes public information.

TRUST

A trust is an excellent way to **ARMOR UP** what you own, dictate where it goes, and keep it private. A trust allows you to specify who inherits what, how much, and when. You can customize it to fit your wishes. However, it must be prepared properly to be legally valid.

Some attorneys may use scare tactics to pressure you into buying a trust, claiming that without one, you'll pay excessive taxes or lose everything to nursing home costs. That's simply not true. For example, one of my clients, a widow with a $200,000 condo, encountered a local attorney who intimidated her into thinking she needed a trust for her condo, and he was ready to charge $2,500 for his services.

Thankfully, like many of my clients, she called me to confirm. I reviewed her situation with our in-house attorney, and we agreed she didn't need what this attorney was pushing. My client did want a trust, but for her specific needs, we created one for just $100. Having a reliable team of experts makes a huge difference.

If you have significant assets and need additional privacy or protection, you may want to consider a marital trust. These can provide exemptions between spouses. These are all great topics we can discuss in detail during a meeting.

YOUR CHANCE TO EVALUATE YOURSELF

Rate your level of concern by circling 1-10. A rank of 1-6 indicates you have a level of concern. An 8, 9 or 10 means you have no concern.

Asset Transfer	*Estate Plan*	1	2	3	4	5	6	8	9	10

- We or I know our assets will transfer according to our wishes when we're gone.
- We have a will and/or trust(s) in place and it's been updated within the last 3 years and it is properly funded.
- Our estate plan is coordinated with our retirement plan to maximize benefits and lower taxes.

Scan the code below to listen to Don's recap

RISK MANAGEMENT INVESTING

Investments For Asset Growth And Preservation

"The hidden cost of turnover (the manager buying and selling) in mutual funds can cost an investor up to 2.4 percent."
—JOHN BOGLE, FOUNDER OF VANGUARD MUTUAL FUNDS

The first "R" in ARMOR. Risk Management - Investing Preservation, Life Stages of Money and Investment Worlds and Understanding Variable Annuities.

A CLOSER LOOK AT MUTUAL FUNDS AND INVESTING STRATEGIES

Since many retirement-minded individuals invest in the stock market, it's important to understand some truths about investing—especially mutual funds. My goal here is not to overwhelm you with details but to give you enough information to think critically and make informed decisions.

MUTUAL FUNDS AND HIDDEN COSTS

Let's start with an idea shared by John Bogle, founder of Vanguard: most investors don't realize the hidden costs of mutual fund managers constantly buying and selling stocks.

Here's a question: **Did you know the average U.S. large-cap mutual fund has a 94% turnover ratio?** That means if a fund holds 100 stocks, the manager replaces about 94 of them annually. This high turnover can cost investors approximately **2.4% annually**—a hidden expense that doesn't have to be disclosed under current regulations.

Let's break it down:

- **Fund size:** $1 billion
- **Turnover rate:** 94%
- **Your investment:** $100,000
- **Cost to you:** $100,000 x 94% = $94,000 x 2.4% = **$2,256 annually**.

These hidden costs can subtly erode your investment returns. Have you ever noticed your account value dropping, even though you've received a 1099 for capital gains or dividends? High turnover could be the culprit, especially if you're relying on these accounts for income. So, how can you address this? Education is key. That's why I collaborate with a broad network of independent advisors nationwide who attend symposiums and stay on top of the latest industry insights. This helps us uncover any hidden costs, expenses, or fees that might be affecting your investments. As a fiduciary advisor, I'm committed to ensuring that both of us stay fully informed.

MYTHS ABOUT MUTUAL FUNDS

Let's address some common myths surrounding mutual funds and investing:

1. **The Myth of Reported Returns**
   Reported returns and what you actually earn are often different. Most investors sense this, but they don't know how to uncover the discrepancy. Just a few paragraphs ago, you learned how to calculate one cost.

2. **The Myth of "Past Performance"**
   Past performance is just that—history. It's commonly believed that funds that performed well in the past will continue to do well in the future. Many investors rely on this assumption when making decisions. However, there's overwhelming evidence showing that past performance doesn't reliably predict future results. If you'd like more information, I can point you in the right direction. This topic is too broad for this book, but I'm happy to discuss it one-on-one.

3. **The Myth of Chasing Returns**
   Chasing returns is a dangerous cycle. Investors often leave underperforming funds to jump into the latest "hot" fund, only to watch that fund decline as well. Fund values typically go through cycles—up, then down. This "buy high, sell low" pattern is a surefire way to lose money, and I can help you map out why this happens.

4. **The Myth of the "Great" Fund Manager**
   Here's a fun one: there are countless stories of "dart-throwing monkeys" outperforming highly paid fund managers. In 2009, a monkey named Lusha outperformed top money managers over 90% of the time. The point? No one, not even the so-called "great" managers, has a consistent track record of beating the market.

5. **The Hidden Loser Fund Myth**
   Some mutual funds hide underperforming funds by merging them into stronger funds, or they close them altogether. You may have encountered this situation. It's unfortunate, but it's something we need to stay vigilant about.

6. **The Market Timing Myth**
   Market timing is one of the most tempting myths. The idea of getting in and out of the market based on predictions sounds appealing, but the reality is that market timing doesn't consistently improve returns—unless you're lucky. Many have fallen victim to this belief. Data consistently shows that market timing, especially when driven by gut instinct, doesn't work. Even legendary fund manager Peter Lynch said, "Attempting to forecast whether the market is at a peak or in a valley is a waste of time."

   For example, from 1984 to 2000, the best years in the history of the Dow Jones occurred, and most investors made their largest gains during that period. Ironically, that was when Peter Lynch was managing Fidelity Magellan, but this kind of success is the exception, not the rule.

WHY DO STOCKBROKERS KEEP PUSHING THESE MYTHS?

Stock-picking, market-timing, and relying on past performance have all been proven to lower returns. So why do so many stockbrokers continue to push these strategies? The answer is simple: they make money off the fees generated by all the trading and buying/selling.

As a conservative advisor focused on retirement planning, I want to make sure you understand the risks involved, even within well-diversified portfolios. My goal is to help you avoid the dangers that can quietly erode your retirement savings.

BUY-AND-HOLD: A FLAWED STRATEGY

The classic "buy-and-hold" strategy has been touted for decades, but it has significant limitations, especially for retirees. While it may work during bull markets, it falters in flat or declining markets—precisely when retirees need stability the most.

Brokers often recommend buy-and-hold because it's easy for them and generates consistent commissions. But this strategy doesn't account for your specific needs, especially as you approach or enter retirement. The question to ask is: **"Hold until when?"**

At Ross Wealth Advisors, we focus on creating strategies to protect your assets and help you transition from growth-focused investing to preservation and income generation.

DOLLAR COST AVERAGING

Dollar cost averaging, a common accumulation strategy, involves regularly investing a fixed amount of money into a fund over time. While this approach has worked for some investors during their earning years, it's less effective for those nearing or in retirement.

The problem arises when you begin withdrawing funds during periods of high market volatility, a phenomenon known as **Reverse Dollar Cost Averaging**. This can accelerate the depletion of your savings and jeopardize your long-term financial security.

A SMARTER APPROACH

Instead of relying on outdated strategies or chasing elusive market gains, focus on a comprehensive plan tailored to your retirement goals. At Ross Wealth Advisors, our **ARMOR UP** approach emphasizes asset protection, income generation, and reducing unnecessary risks.

We'll discuss these concepts in greater detail later, but the key takeaway is this: understanding the myths, costs, and risks of traditional investing strategies can empower you to make better decisions. Your retirement deserves a strategy built for your unique needs—not one designed to benefit Wall Street.

PRESERVATION
It's About Preserving And Enjoying

"In all things, success depends on previous preparation, and without such preparation, there is to be such failure."
—CONFUCIUS

DEFINING ASSET SAFETY AND RISK: THE RULE OF 100

Every day, I meet retirement-minded individuals whose lifetime savings are exposed to significant market risk. While the stock market can offer growth, the closer you are to retirement—or already retired—the more critical it becomes to balance risk and safety.

One tool I often reference to help clients understand the appropriate balance of safety and risk is **DR's Rule of 100**.

How the Rule of 100 Works

Take your age and subtract it from 100. The result represents the maximum percentage of your retirement savings that should be invested in riskier assets. For example:

- If you're 65 years old, subtract 65 from 100.
- The result, 35, is the percentage of your portfolio that can be allocated to at-risk investments like stocks or mutual funds.

Conversely, the remaining **65%** of your retirement savings should be in safer, guaranteed assets with limited market risk. These safer, also alternative, investments can provide reliable cash flow during retirement and help **ARMOR UP** your retirement plan. Note: This is a rule of thumb, not always mandatory.

Green Money vs. Red Money

- **Green Money:** This is the safe portion of your portfolio—assets that are guaranteed or protected from market fluctuations, as well as other alternative investments.
- **Red Money:** This represents the at-risk portion—investments subject to market volatility.

As a general rule, the older you are, the more conservative your portfolio should be. By gradually shifting a larger percentage of your assets into Green Money, you reduce the chance of a significant loss that could derail your retirement plans. Again, this is always case by case and different for everyone.

The Risk of Being Overexposed

If too much of your retirement savings is in Red Money, a sudden market downturn could substantially reduce your nest egg. Even a temporary drop could create an income gap, forcing you to adjust your lifestyle or withdraw more than planned. This situation not only impacts your financial security but can also lead to unnecessary stress—when you should be enjoying the freedom retirement brings.

Are You Properly ARMORED UP?

Take a moment to reflect:

- Would your retirement plan withstand a significant market decline?
- Could you afford to lose a large portion of the assets you're relying on for income in your retirement years?

If you're unsure, it may be time to reassess your portfolio and ensure your retirement savings are aligned with your goals and tolerance for risk. The Rule of 100 is a starting point, but a personalized strategy can provide the clarity and confidence you need to enjoy retirement to the fullest.

TWO QUESTIONS ABOUT YOUR RETIREMENT FUNDS

What percentage of your money is red money, or money at risk?

1. **What percentage of your money is red money, or money at risk?**
2. **What percentage of your money is green, safe money?**

When I look at retirement-minded folks' portfolios, many, unfortunately, have **85–95%** in red (at-risk) money and only **10–15%** in green (safer) money. That is upside down, in my opinion. When I meet with people looking for a plan of action, it is not uncommon to see several couples or individuals a week who are invested as if they are still thirty years old, taking on far too much risk at this stage of life.

As an independent fiduciary advisor, my goal is to educate people on how to create more cash flow from their hard-earned retirement savings and safely **ARMOR UP** to protect it from unnecessary risk.

Again, most of my clients and prospective clients are retirement-minded, and for them, the **Buy-and-Hold strategy** in equities (for all their retirement savings) does not work anymore. For one thing, they no longer have the salary that supports a dollar-cost averaging program, such as systematic savings through payroll deduction into a 401(k). In general, their "risk tolerance" is much lower.

When a retiree begins to use his or her retirement savings as intended, and that account is primarily in securities (exposed to downside risk), they are in a situation called **"reverse dollar-cost averaging."**

If you retire and stop adding money to your retirement account, but instead begin withdrawing income from it during a market downturn, you will experience the principle of reverse dollar-cost averaging. Not only is the market going down, but you are withdrawing funds, which means you're taking more principal out just to maintain the same income level.

For example, if you are drawing 6% annually, and the market declines by 10%, you're depleting principal. You will need to withdraw even more to maintain that 6% income flow. This is called reverse dollar-cost averaging, and it's something the marketing people and sales reps on Wall Street don't like to discuss.

My Concern

If you're taking money to live on from an account that goes up and down, you run the risk of **running out of money**. No one wants that! My clients learn how to create their own **"personal pension."** Running out of money consistently ranks as one of the top retirement fears.

We use a powerful software program called the **Retirement Income Analyzer**.

Together, we can review different scenarios for your individual situation. We will talk about your comfort level with risk and how much money you need to live on to enjoy turning your **paycheck into a playcheck**.

NOTE: These charts are difficult to read in book format and are just used here as a snapshot view. We're able to put your scenarios up on our big conference screen.

Retirement Assessment - Running Out of Money

Year	His Age	Her Age	Pension Income	Security Income	Monthly Cash Flows	Annual Cash Flows	Net Monthly Income	Net Monthly Expenses	Net Monthly Cash Flow	Annuity Acct Value	Protected Assets	Spendable Assets
										$0	$152,792	$975,694
2023	66	66	$0	$4,731	$0	$0	$4,731	$7,601	$2,870	$0	$152,792	$993,348
2024	67	67	$0	$4,844	$0	$0	$4,844	$7,850	$3,006	$0	$152,792	$1,022,946
2025	68	68	$0	$4,961	$0	$0	$4,961	$8,107	$3,146	$0	$152,792	$1,047,571
2026	69	69	$0	$5,080	$0	$0	$5,080	$8,372	$3,292	$0	$152,792	$1,069,415
2027	70	70	$0	$5,202	$0	$0	$5,202	$8,645	$3,443	$0	$152,792	$1,088,894
2028	71	71	$0	$5,326	$0	$0	$5,326	$8,928	$3,602	$0	$152,792	$1,105,859
2029	72	72	$0	$5,454	$0	$0	$5,453	$9,220	$3,767	$0	$152,792	$1,119,986
2030	73	73	$0	$5,585	$0	$0	$5,583	$9,522	$3,939	$0	$152,792	$1,130,876
2031	74	74	$0	$5,719	$0	$0	$5,715	$9,833	$4,118	$0	$152,792	$1,138,660
2032	75	75	$0	$5,857	$0	$0	$5,852	$10,154	$4,302	$0	$152,792	$1,143,649
2033	76	76	$0	$5,997	$0	$0	$5,991	$10,486	$4,495	$0	$152,792	$1,145,528
2034	77	77	$0	$6,141	$0	$0	$6,133	$10,829	$4,696	$0	$152,792	$1,143,839
2035	78	78	$0	$6,288	$0	$0	$6,279	$11,184	$4,905	$0	$152,792	$1,137,548
2036	79	79	$0	$6,439	$0	$0	$6,428	$11,549	$5,121	$0	$152,792	$1,125,886
2037	80	80	$0	$6,594	$0	$0	$6,582	$11,927	$5,345	$0	$152,792	$1,108,911
2038	81	81	$0	$6,752	$0	$0	$6,738	$12,317	$5,579	$0	$152,792	$1,086,445
2039	82	82	$0	$6,914	$0	$0	$6,899	$12,720	$5,821	$0	$152,792	$1,058,070
2040	83	83	$0	$7,080	$0	$0	$7,063	$13,136	$6,073	$0	$152,792	$1,023,281
2041	84	84	$0	$7,250	$0	$0	$7,232	$12,386	$5,154	$0	$152,792	$995,914
2042	85	85	$0	$7,424	$0	$0	$7,403	$12,791	$5,388	$0	$152,792	$966,138
2043	86	86	$0	$7,602	$0	$0	$7,578	$13,210	$5,632	$0	$152,792	$930,921
2044	87	87	$0	$7,785	$0	$0	$7,758	$13,642	$5,884	$0	$152,792	$889,075
2045	88	88	$0	$7,971	$0	$0	$7,941	$14,088	$6,147	$0	$152,792	$839,819
2046	89	89	$0	$8,163	$0	$0	$8,130	$14,548	$6,418	$0	$152,792	$782,489
2047	90	90	$0	$8,359	$0	$0	$8,323	$15,024	$6,701	$0	$152,792	$716,378
2048	91	91	$0	$8,559	$0	$0	$8,520	$15,515	$6,995	$0	$152,792	$640,742
2049	92	92	$0	$8,765	$0	$0	$8,722	$16,023	$7,301	$0	$152,792	$554,803
2050	93	93	$0	$8,975	$0	$0	$8,929	$16,547	$7,618	$0	$152,792	$457,708
2051	94	94	$0	$9,191	$0	$0	$9,141	$17,088	$7,947	$0	$152,792	$348,566
2052	95	95	$0	$9,411	$0	$0	$9,358	$17,647	$8,289	$0	$152,792	$226,306
2053	96	96	$0	$9,637	$0	$0	$9,580	$18,224	$8,644	$0	$152,792	$89,784
2054	97	97	$0	$9,868	$0	$0	$9,807	$18,819	$9,012	$0	$152,792	$0
2055	98	98	$0	$10,105	$0	$0	$10,041	$19,435	$9,394	$0	$152,792	$0
2056	99	99	$0	$10,348	$0	$0	$10,280	$20,070	$9,790	$0	$152,792	$0
2057	100	100	$0	$10,596	$0	$0	$10,524	$20,727	$10,203	$0	$152,792	$0

The chart above shows a prospective client running out of money with their current plan.

Retirement Assessment - NOT Running Out of Money

Year	His Age	Her Age	Pension Income	Security Income	Monthly Cash Flows	Annual Cash Flows	Net Monthly Income	Net Monthly Expenses	Net Monthly Cash Flow	Annuity Acct Value	Protected Assets	Spendable Assets
										$0	$152,792	$475,694
2023	66	66	$0	$4,731	$3,682	$0	$8,240	$7,601	$639	$0	$152,792	$500,673
2024	67	67	$0	$4,844	$3,682	$0	$7,879	$7,850	$29	$0	$152,792	$538,858
2025	68	68	$0	$4,961	$3,682	$0	$7,988	$8,107	-$119	$0	$152,792	$578,048
2026	69	69	$0	$5,080	$3,682	$0	$8,099	$8,372	-273	$0	$152,792	$618,177
2027	70	70	$0	$5,202	$3,682	$0	$8,213	$8,645	-432	$0	$152,792	$658,872
2028	71	71	$0	$5,326	$3,682	$0	$8,329	$8,928	-599	$0	$152,792	$699,820
2029	72	72	$0	$5,454	$3,682	$0	$8,448	$9,220	-772	$0	$152,792	$740,855
2030	73	73	$0	$5,585	$3,682	$0	$8,570	$9,522	-952	$0	$152,792	$781,826
2031	74	74	$0	$5,719	$3,682	$0	$8,695	$9,833	-1,138	$0	$152,792	$816,624
2032	75	75	$0	$5,857	$3,682	$0	$8,824	$10,154	-1,330	$0	$152,792	$854,736
2033	76	76	$0	$5,997	$3,682	$0	$8,954	$10,486	-1,532	$0	$152,792	$893,172
2034	77	77	$0	$6,141	$3,682	$0	$9,089	$10,82	-1,740	$0	$152,792	$930,776
2035	78	78	$0	$6,288	$3,682	$0	$9,226	$11,18	-$1,958	$0	$152,792	$966,509
2036	79	79	$0	$6,439	$3,682	$0	$9,367	$11,549	-$2,182	$0	$152,792	$999,636
2037	80	80	$0	$6,594	$3,682	$0	$9,511	$11,927	-$2,416	$0	$152,792	$1,030,337
2038	81	81	$0	$6,752	$3,682	$0	$9,659	$12,317	-$2,658	$0	$152,792	$1,058,471
2039	82	82	$0	$6,914	$3,682	$0	$9,810	$12,720	-$2,910	$0	$152,792	$1,083,689
2040	83	83	$0	$7,080	$3,682	$0	$9,965	$13,136	-$3,171	$0	$152,792	$1,105,564
2041	84	84	$0	$7,250	$3,682	$0	$10,123	$12,386	-$2,263	$0	$152,792	$1,138,159
2042	85	85	$0	$7,424	$3,682	$0	$10,285	$12,791	-$2,506	$0	$152,792	$1,171,957
2043	86	86	$0	$7,602	$3,682	$0	$10,451	$13,210	-$2,759	$0	$152,792	$1,204,072
2044	87	87	$0	$7,785	$3,682	$0	$10,622	$13,642	$3,020	$0	$152,792	$1,233,434
2045	88	88	$0	$7,971	$3,682	$0	$10,796	$14,088	-$3,292	$0	$152,792	$1,259,382
2046	89	89	$0	$8,163	$3,682	$0	$10,975	$14,548	-$3,573	$0	$152,792	$1,281,360
2047	90	90	$0	$8,359	$3,682	$0	$11,157	$15,024	-$3,867	$0	$152,792	$1,298,766
2048	91	91	$0	$8,559	$3,682	$0	$11,344	$15,515	-$4,171	$0	$152,792	$1,310,949
2049	92	92	$0	$8,765	$3,682	$0	$11,536	$16,023	-$4,487	$0	$152,792	$1,317,208
2050	93	93	$0	$8,975	$3,682	$0	$11,732	$16,547	-$4,815	$0	$152,792	$1,316,760
2051	94	94	$0	$9,191	$3,682	$0	$11,933	$17,088	-$5,155	$0	$152,792	$1,308,760
2052	95	95	$0	$9,411	$3,682	$0	$12,139	$17,647	-$5,508	$0	$152,792	$1,292,162
2053	96	96	$0	$9,637	$3,682	$0	$12,349	$18,224	-$5,875	$0	$152,792	$1,266,534
2054	97	97	$0	$9,868	$3,682	$0	$12,565	$18,819	-$6,254	$0	$152,792	$1,232,326
2055	98	98	$0	$10,105	$3,682	$0	$12,786	$19,435	-$6,649	$0	$152,792	$1,188,748
2056	99	99	$0	$10,	$3,682	$0	$13,013	$20,070	-$7,057	$0	$152,792	$1,134,962
2057	100	10	0 $	0 $1	$3,682	$0	$13,244	$20,727	-$7,483	$0	$152,792	$1,070,053

The chart above shows the same person, but this person does not run out of money with my plan and recommendations. The sixth column illustrates the "personal pension" we created.

That's the situation if your portfolio continues to contain all equity holdings (stocks and mutual funds). That is what could happen if you continue with the approach you used during your income-earning (working) years, even though you have stopped working. This is true, even though you may not actually be buying any more equities, because your money remains tied up in the equities you purchased when you were more risk-tolerant (during your working years).

Most people who have all or most of their money in their 401(k), by definition, have their money exposed to the everyday Wall Street risk of the volatile up-or-down markets. About 80 to 90 percent of retirement accounts that I see have a majority of investments in stocks because that is where they were in the 401(k)s.

RETIREMENT PORTFOLIO OR A WORKING PERSON'S PORTFOLIO?

In some ways, I cannot blame people for shifting out of the workforce and into retirement with a portfolio that looks like a working person's portfolio. Many people do not think there is a need for a strategic change once they retire. Remember the stock market of the 1980s and 1990s? Most people who were working during those years made most of their money during that stretch of time. Those were some of the best years for the market.

UNDERSTANDING THE CHART

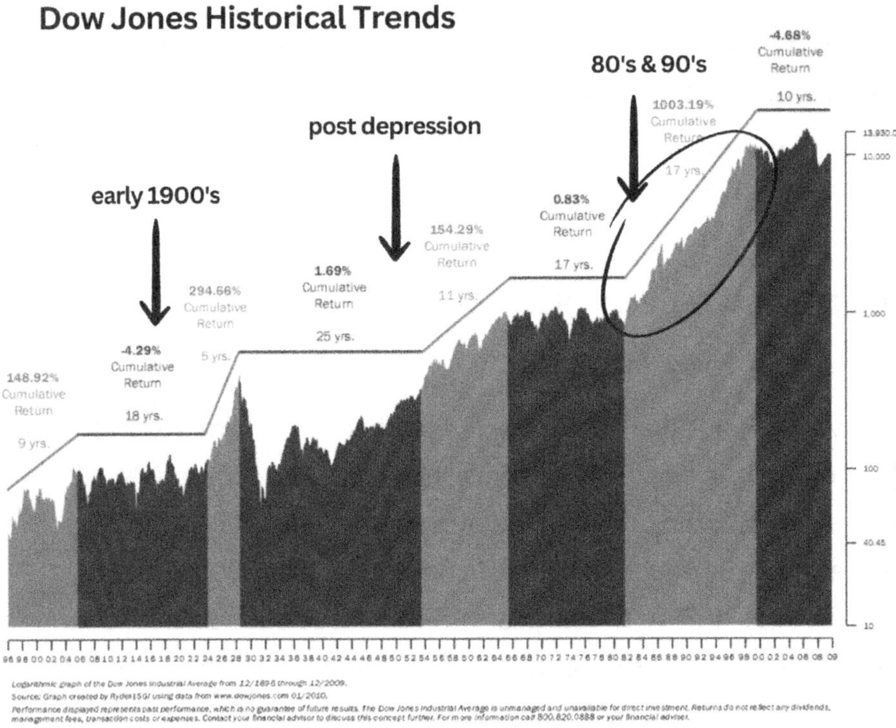

Many people assumed the soaring returns of the 1980s and 1990s were the norm—high returns, a climbing stock market, and mutual funds delivering impressive gains. Unfortunately, we're now living in a different reality, and it's far from the "good old days" of those decades.

On the day of retirement, people often celebrate by cleaning out their cubicles, sending final emails, and high-fiving coworkers. It's a well-deserved milestone, worthy of celebration. However, what also deserves attention is the shift in how retirees should approach their retirement savings. Once you walk out of the office, the rules change, and so should your strategy.

Who's Advising You?

If you have a 401(k), you likely don't have a dedicated advisor. You may recall someone from the 401(k) company coming in once a year to answer questions, but that's not financial advice.

Many 401(k) plans are managed by large mutual fund companies like Fidelity or Vanguard. These companies are Wall Street firms primarily focused on selling mutual funds. When you retire, they often want to continue managing your money by rolling your 401(k) into an IRA. But while your circumstances and risk tolerance have changed, your investments may not. These brokers often leave your portfolio allocated the same way it was when you were working.

Changing Needs, Changing Strategy

Retirement is a significant life change, and your investments should reflect that. As your needs evolve, so too should the way your money is invested. Unfortunately, many retirees aren't properly advised or attempt to manage their investments themselves. I've met with many "do-it-yourselfers," and I can often see the concern in their spouse's eyes. "What if they make a mistake? What do we do then?"

Risk vs. Reward

Here's what I tell my clients and prospective clients: **there is no free lunch on Wall Street.** If you're a conservative investor, you should limit your exposure to individual stocks and equity mutual funds, especially for generating a guaranteed income. Protecting your principal while earning a reasonable return is critical. If your principal is exposed to inappropriate risk, you're no longer investing—you're gambling.

Would you take your life savings to Las Vegas? Many retirees unknowingly gamble their savings by keeping too much of their portfolio in risky Wall Street investments. While some equity exposure is important, it must be structured properly for long-term growth or inheritance goals.

Buy-and-Hold: A Risky Roller-Coaster

Consider the Buy-and-Hold strategy. If you've owned stocks or mutual funds, you know they can—and do—go down in value. Let's look at October 2007, the peak before the 2008 market crash. As the market declined, many advisors failed to recommend moving to safer investments. Why? Because keeping assets in equities generated fees and commissions for them.

Instead of having an exit strategy, clients were told to "ride it out." This approach left retirees hoping the market would rebound in time for their withdrawals. But hope is not a strategy. Gains on Wall Street aren't truly yours until you take the money out of the market, just like casino chips aren't yours until you cash them in.

For retirees, the stakes are higher. Unlike during your working years, when paychecks and time could help you recover from losses, a significant downturn can jeopardize your retirement savings.

The Need for Principal Protection

Retirees today face additional challenges, such as cuts to pensions and the risk of insolvency in municipal pension plans. For example, the city of Stockton, California, declared bankruptcy in 2012, leaving many workers' pensions in jeopardy. Those workers needed principal-protected investments to replace lost income.

This is why retirement-minded individuals must **ARMOR UP** their savings. Protecting your nest egg is essential, and the time to act is now.

THE PRESERVATION AND ENJOYMENT STAGE

Once you retire, you enter a whole new stage of life: the **Preservation and Enjoyment stage**. You've worked hard to get here, so protecting and preserving your nest egg is critical. If a few poor decisions result in significant losses, the game can be over.

Many advisors don't call retirees to urge them to capture gains, leading investors to continue with a buy-and-hold strategy. Gains are often made on paper but then given back when the market declines, and the cycle repeats because they aren't selling.

The way to succeed in the markets is to buy low and sell high. However, most retirees aren't day traders sitting at their computers all day. For one, day trading is risky, and retirees have far more enjoyable ways to spend their time—traveling, visiting grandkids, or taking classes at the university. Unfortunately, too many retirees rely on the hope that the market will go up, a mindset that can be disastrous for retirement accounts. That's why I work to educate people to think differently as they enter this stage of life.

A Poor Approach

I often hear prospective clients admit that when their quarterly brokerage statement arrives, they only look at the front page to see if their retirement accounts went up or down. They pay little or no attention to the remaining pages. This is not a sound strategy for someone in retirement—it's certainly not a plan for abundance.

Now is the time to seek **reliable, proven alternative investments** that provide more secure methods to **ARMOR UP** your retirement. Keeping all your savings in Wall Street investments at this stage is akin to gambling at a casino. I'd rather see you enjoy your money with a plan that ensures you'll have enough for the rest of your life.

Lessons From the Past

I remember many people nearing retirement in 2000 when the market crashed due to the tech bubble. Technology stocks that fueled the "dot-com bubble" were hit especially hard.

If you had sold your technology-heavy portfolio in February 2000, before the crash, you might have been one of the fortunate ones, selling near the NASDAQ Composite's peak of 5,132. On the other hand, those who waited until after the crash, when the NASDAQ dropped to less than 2,500, faced a very different reality.

I've met many prospective clients who lost **40–50% of their life savings** during that crash and had to delay retirement or keep working because they could no longer afford to stop.

A Real-World Example

I worked with several Lucent Technologies employees during this time. In the early 2000s, Lucent stock (LU) was soaring, and many employees had **100% of their 401(k) invested in it**.

I advised my clients, "Just in case the stock drops, let's sell half of your shares and move them into safer, retirement-focused investments." Those who followed this advice were thrilled they joined Ross Wealth Advisors, as they avoided significant losses when the stock plummeted.

Unfortunately, not everyone heeded my advice. One prospective client I remember well declined to work with us, saying, "I thought you might be too expensive." At the time, his 401(k) was valued at $500,000, all in Lucent stock. By the end of the decline in 2002, his 401(k) was worth around **$10,000**.

My services wouldn't have cost him $490,000. It's heartbreaking to see situations like this, where a little time spent planning could have **ARMORed UP** their retirement savings and protected their financial future.

WHAT CAN YOU LEARN FROM A MOUNTAIN CLIMBING EXPEDITION?

If you think of your career as a long mountain climb, imagine the various stages representing your journey. Along the way, you experience beautiful scenery, perhaps a rainstorm, followed by a rockslide, then a valley with a pristine waterfall. Finally, you reach the last few miles of this great adventure. Your hard work has paid off, and now you've reached the summit—**retirement!**

From the summit, you begin your initial descent, followed by a gradual slope, and ultimately, you arrive safely at base camp.

WHEN DO MOST CLIMBING ACCIDENTS HAPPEN?

Whenever possible, I like to start discussions with clients at or before they begin their "initial descent" into retirement. More frequently now, people are reaching out before they hit the peak of their careers, allowing us to prepare early. This preparation maximizes retirement savings and enables us to implement strategic tax reduction strategies.

By the way, do you know when most accidents happen on mountain climbing expeditions? Correct—the descent.

There are many options for people in their fifties or around age sixty. For example, a couple recently came in to talk with me. Both were enjoying successful careers and were sixty years old. They said, "We're planning to work until about age sixty-three. We want to start working with you now to protect our retirement accounts from potential losses before we retire."

"Perfect timing," I said. "Let's get started. Just like with mountain climbers, my absolute priority is **safety**. We do not want a fall during the descent. Our focus will be on your **financial safety**. Together, we'll decide what portion of your assets should be protected and no longer subjected to risk. These funds will be needed for cash flow and will come from savings vehicles. And just because money is protected from risk doesn't mean it has to be in an account earning little to nothing."

One final thought on the mountain climbing metaphor: climbing to the top of a mountain is optional, but coming down safely is **mandatory**. Similarly, taking risks with your savings and investments is optional, but ensuring you don't run out of money in retirement is **mandatory**.

SECOND OPINIONS ON OUR HEALTH AND SECOND OPINIONS ON OUR WEALTH

We get second opinions for our health, so doesn't it make sense to get a second opinion on our wealth? Importantly, that second opinion can't come from the person who gave you the first one—sometimes that's your current advisor.

Many people have spent their entire lives saving, often through brokerage firms, resulting in 401(k)s or IRAs fully invested in stocks or mutual funds. But how many are receiving advice on risk reduction or the Rule of 100? This is your net worth—a lifetime's work—and it must be protected and preserved to last through retirement.

The Rule of 100 is a helpful guideline, but it's not a rigid plan. Each individual has a unique risk tolerance, and the only way to establish proper investment priorities is by working with an advisor experienced in retirement planning.

Even those who avoided downside market risk in the past may have faced another challenge: inflation. As prices rose, their purchasing power declined. The same monthly check began buying less at the supermarket, and that's a reality a good financial plan must address.

In my approach, I show clients the options available for their dollars, including safe-money investments. Certificates of deposit (CDs) often pay less than 1%, failing to keep up with inflation, but there are other hybrid accounts that offer safety, guarantees, and above-average returns.

We can explore these secure options, used by many of my clients and millions of others nationwide, to ensure their savings aren't affected by market volatility or the economy. That's the **ARMOR UP** strategy for an abundant retirement.

Each client's needs, goals, and dreams are unique, and we work together to build the best retirement plan to meet them.

LIFE STAGES OF MONEY & INVESTMENT WORLDS

"If your retirement represents a fundamental change in life, shouldn't your investments?"

—DON ROSS

SAFETY RISK OR IN BETWEEN? HOW TO PROTECT AND ALLOCATE YOUR FUNDS

This chapter focuses on strategies for protecting and allocating your funds as you prepare for and navigate retirement.

The Three Worlds

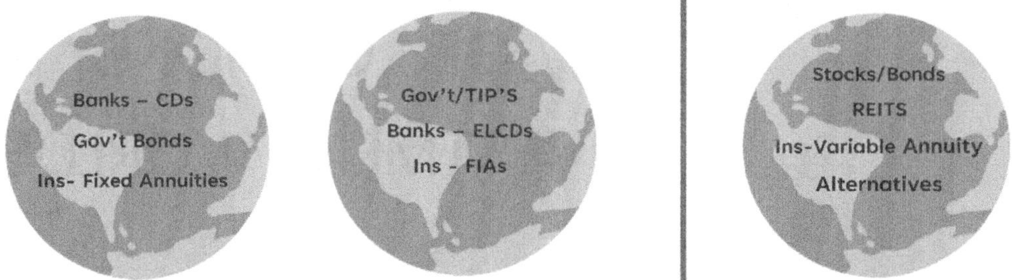

Safety/Guarantees	Hybrid	Risk/Potential Growth
- Principle is guaranteed - Interest is guaranteed - Penalties for early w/drawl	- Principal Protection - Interest linked to external market index - Not invested directly in market	- Principal is not guaranteed - Interest/earnings NOT guaranteed - Term is generally open ended - Need TIME to be effective
Potential 12 Months Interest **1% - 2%**	**Potential 12 Months Interest** **0% - 5%**	**Potential 12 Months Interest** **-40% - +40%**

The chart above, called **The Three Worlds**, illustrates how I believe assets should be allocated for those approaching or living in retirement.

Starting with the **Safety and Guarantees** bucket on the left: this is where you keep funds in a safe place for quick access. Ideally, you should set aside six to twelve months of expenses for emergencies. This is similar to when you received your first paycheck and likely deposited it in a bank for safekeeping. While this bucket offers safety and guarantees, it typically yields very little.

Key features of banks, bonds, or fixed annuities in the Safety bucket:

- **Low yield**
- **Principal and interest guarantees**
- **Specific rules for accessing funds**
- **Early withdrawal penalties**

The Safety bucket is essential for preserving money that might be needed immediately, and these funds are often held by banks or similar institutions.

The second bucket is the **Risk** bucket, associated with growth. This stage aligns with your working years when you begin saving beyond your emergency fund. These funds are used for long-term growth, like building savings for retirement.

Many people enjoy taking advantage of the stock market's growth potential. I often say the stock market is the greatest wealth-creation tool ever. While it comes with risk, it's well-suited for wealth-building during your twenties, thirties, forties, and even fifties.

Key features of the Risk bucket:

- **Risk of losing your principal**
- **No guaranteed dividends or interest**
- **Significant growth potential over time**

The growth potential of these investments makes them attractive for long-term goals. While they are essential for accumulation, they are not always appropriate for generating all of your retirement income.

The Risk bucket includes mutual funds, stocks, bonds, ETFs, options, and variable annuities. The purpose of these vehicles? **Accumulation**.

WHAT ABOUT REAL ESTATE INVESTMENTS?

I do not include real estate as an investment option here, although many of my clients have used rental properties to generate income and build equity. Rental property is a long-term investment, typically requiring a holding period of 15 to 30 years.

When investing in real estate, you need to be cautious. Tenant turnover can be frequent, and changeover costs can add up quickly. Routine repairs, capital improvements, and renovations are often expensive. The key takeaway is that rental properties are a **"lifestyle" investment**.

Being a landlord isn't for everyone. Rental properties are time-intensive, and owning them is much like running a business. You must be available 24/7 for emergencies or hire a property manager, which adds to your expenses.

Most people dislike being constantly contacted about tenant issues, property maintenance, or even dealing with evictions for non-payment of rent. For these reasons, real estate investments aren't practical for everyone.

TIME: THE KEY ISSUE WITH THE RISK BUCKET

The main concern with the Risk Bucket is that it requires **time**. You need time for investments to grow and time to recover from market downturns. But how much time does a 65-year-old—or an 80-year-old—really have?

This becomes especially critical when these funds are needed for month-to-month living expenses. Any losses can lead to significant lifestyle changes, which no one wants.

It's also important to understand that losses **hurt twice as much as gains help**. That's why I focus on teaching my clients strategies to **ARMOR UP** their retirement savings.

BUCKET THREE: THE HYBRID

Bucket three, or the Hybrid bucket, includes financial instruments that combine **principal protection** (like bucket one) with **growth potential** (like bucket two). However, the Hybrid bucket focuses less on growth and more on **cash flow**.

This distinction—**cash flow**—is the key difference.

The primary instruments in the Hybrid bucket include **Indexed CDs, TIPS** and **Indexed Annuities**. We'll discuss Indexed Annuities in a later chapter, as they are an essential tool to consider when planning to **ARMOR UP** your retirement.

In the Hybrid bucket, **cash flow** refers to guarantees that provide retirees with the safety and income they need. The insurance industry continues to develop new products designed specifically to offer these guarantees.

Depending on your situation, the features of the right hybrid account could be invaluable to your plan.

Later, I'll explain how we structure income plans that provide retirees with **guaranteed cash flow**—ensuring peace of mind, regardless of economic conditions. Many retirees find this approach appealing for protecting and securing their retirement savings.

It's important to understand that every financial tool serves a specific purpose. Many people mistakenly believe they are diversified because they own 15 different mutual funds. This is not true diversification for a solid retirement income plan. In fact, this kind of "diversification" could lead to significant losses during a market downturn due to a lack of proper asset allocation.

Note: We'll discuss the Life Stages—or what I call the Three Worlds of Money—in much greater detail when we meet face-to-face. This is a critical conversation for positioning your savings and investments effectively for retirement.

UNDERSTANDING VARIABLE ANNUITIES

Let me start by sharing my feelings about Variable Annuities: I'm not a fan. A Variable Annuity is essentially a Wall Street product wrapped in an insurance policy, and in my opinion, it gives investors a false sense of security.

Recently, I spoke to a group of retirement-minded individuals and explained why I believe Variable Annuities are not suitable for their stage of life. One attendee, a widow (I work with many widows), decided to call her Variable Annuity company before our consultation to ask about the fees I had discussed. She was shocked by what she discovered. While these products offer some guarantees, the cost of obtaining those guarantees is very high, and the numerous fees make it hard to see meaningful returns. In most cases, the market must return 3–5% annually just to break even. Once you invest in a Variable Annuity, getting out can be challenging. That's why I advise my clients to avoid them.

High Costs and Market Volatility

In the 1980s and 1990s, with a booming market, it was easier to overcome the high fees associated with Variable Annuities. But in today's volatile markets, if you need income, these products can be a significant risk. Wall Street firms and banks are still selling Variable Annuities at record levels, but investors need to be cautious.

Variable Annuities often use the names of reputable insurance companiesT, but don't be misled—they are still Wall Street products. These annuities come with a prospectus, which means they are registered securities with two critical implications:

1. There are fees.
2. You can lose your principal.

Why Not Choose Safer Alternatives?

You can allocate your money into mutual funds within a Variable Annuity, but those sub-accounts don't offer guarantees. Alternatively, you could choose a fixed account with a guaranteed minimum interest rate, but few people do because the return is minimal.

If you're considering a fixed rate option, you're likely better off purchasing a fixed annuity without the fees or loads that come with Variable Annuities. Brokers selling Variable Annuities often don't recommend these alternatives because Variable Annuities pay higher commissions. Essentially, Variable Annuities are mutual funds wrapped in an expensive insurance policy, and you could purchase mutual funds much cheaper outside of an annuity.

A Product of the Bull Market

Variable Annuities became popular during the roaring bull market of the 1990s when people were making significant returns and looking for tax shelters. Gains inside the annuity were tax-deferred, making it appealing at the time. But when the market began to collapse, many investors saw their savings dwindle. My clients, however, with the **ARMOR UP plan**, didn't worry because their savings were structured to preserve and protect against losses.

The Bottom Line

Variable Annuities are heavily laden with fees, often between 3–5% annually, whether your investments gain or lose value. These fees ensure brokers, insurance companies, and back-office staff get paid every year, regardless of your returns. For the investor, this means the market must increase by at least the amount of the fees just to break even. If the market rises by 10%, you're only netting 6% after fees.

While hundreds of billions of dollars in Variable Annuities are sold annually, they primarily benefit brokers and insurance companies—not the investors. My approach focuses on working with clients to **preserve and protect their savings**, ensuring they have a reliable plan for an abundant retirement. Variable Annuities simply don't align with that philosophy.

WHY VARIABLE ANNUITY FEES DO NOT SHOW UP ON YOUR STATEMENT

Many people are unaware of the fees associated with Variable Annuities because they don't show up on their statements—they're buried in the contract. This is why it's essential to read the contract carefully or have it reviewed by a financial professional to understand the hidden costs.

Variable Annuities charge a **mortality and expense fee** due to the death benefit feature. For example, if you invest $100,000 and the market drops 50%, reducing your account value to $50,000, the death benefit guarantees your beneficiaries receive the original $100,000. However, this protection comes with a fee, and it can be misleading.

Additionally, the death benefit payout is fully taxable.

My question is this: why use an accumulation product for retirement? Variable Annuities may be appropriate for someone in their 20s, 30s, 40s, or even 50s. But for a retirement-minded person focused on protecting savings and income, they are not the right choice to **ARMOR UP** your financial future.

TYPICAL VARIABLE ANNUITY FEES

High Fees

M&E..1.50%
Sub Account Ave...................0.96%
Death Benefit ....1.15% (5% rollup)
Income Rider ....1.50% (6% rollup, 5% payout)

$100,000 - $5,110/year in fees, $1,000,000 - $51,100/year in fees, $25,550- over 5 years - $255,000 in fees

A formula to erode your principal quickly

It is my belief the smarter investment is to consider a life insurance policy, if you believe a smarter choice is to consider a life insurance policy, if you qualify. It costs less, and all proceeds are **tax-free** upon death. The Variable Annuity death benefit, on the other hand, often gives a false sense of security. Many think, "I have a death benefit," but the problem arises when you need the money to live on now.

In the market downturn scenario, you'd find yourself living on $50,000 instead of $100,000. The only way to recover the full $100,000 is to die, and even then, it goes to your beneficiary—not you. This is not how life insurance should be used. Life insurance is an excellent tool for protection and estate planning, but it's not suited for an investment plan. There are far better ways to use money in an investment account, and I'll discuss how life insurance can be leveraged effectively in a later chapter.

Here's the reality: with a Variable Annuity, the life insurance company adds a life insurance policy onto your annuity, and you're the one paying for it. That policy typically costs around **1.5% annually** of the annuity's total value. That's just the **mortality and expense cost**. On top of that, there's an administration charge and the cost of the mutual funds, which can range from **1% to 2% per year**. One of the largest hidden costs in mutual funds—whether inside or outside a Variable Annuity—is turnover cost, as previously discussed.

MORE REASONS VARIABLE ANNUITIES COULD BE UNFAIR TO YOU

Variable Annuities often include a **guaranteed income rider**, also called a **living benefit rider**, which can be misleading. For example, your $100,000 investment may be guaranteed to grow at 6%, regardless of market performance. While this sounds appealing, the reality is the rider comes with an additional **1.5%–2% fee**. Add this to the **2% mutual fund fee** and the **1.5% mortality and expense fee**, and you're paying around **5% annually** in costs.

To get the 6% guaranteed growth, most contracts require you to **annuitize**. This means signing over the rights to your cash to the insurance company, forfeiting your ability to withdraw it. Instead, the company pays you back the balance as a lifetime income stream, often with minimal interest.

For example, if the market drops and your account value declines to $50,000, the income rider might show an income value of $150,000. However, you can't cash out the $150,000—you must annuitize to receive it as monthly payments over your lifetime. If you have 20 years left to live, this comes out to about $625 a month. Essentially, you're just getting your principal back over time with little or no growth.

Hidden Costs and Misleading Guarantees

Variable Annuities are marketed heavily by Wall Street and insurance brokers because they generate substantial fees and commissions. Brokers often pitch these products as offering "all the upside of the market" with a "guaranteed 6% growth," but the fine print tells a different story. The 6% is hypothetical, meant for income calculations only, and doesn't represent money you can withdraw.

Many people who purchase Variable Annuities later feel misled, asking, "How do I get out of this?" Unfortunately, during the surrender period, exiting comes with a penalty.

The Importance of Education

When I meet with prospective clients who own Variable Annuities, I often call the insurance company during our meeting. Together, we ask specific questions about the contract, fees, and guarantees. One gentleman, who owned multiple Variable Annuities sold by three different brokers, told me after a single call, "I learned more from you in 18 minutes than I have in 10 years from my brokers." That's the kind of clarity I aim to provide.

At my educational workshops, I invite attendees with Variable Annuities to bring in their contracts for a review. Together, we examine the fees, guarantees, and how the product actually works. Many clients tell me, "The broker never explained this," or, "If I had known this, I never would have bought it."

If you own a Variable Annuity, let me help you explore your options. I've assisted many people in moving out of these products after showing them the details in plain English. My recommendations always prioritize improvement and absolute value—if it's not in your best interest, it's not the right choice.

Contractual Guarantees Matter

The second most important words to a retiree (after **cash flow**) are **contractual guarantee**. These guarantees ensure a certain payout rate for a set time or for life. However, not all insurance companies offer the same rates or terms. Bankers or brokers often represent only one company, limiting your options. I believe that's not in your best interest. My goal is to ensure my clients receive the **highest contractually guaranteed payout** available. Period.

YOUR CHANCE TO EVALUATE YOURSELF

Rate your level of concern by circling 1-10. A rank of 1-6 indicates you have a level of concern. An 8, 9 or 10 means you have no concern.

Risk Management *Investing* 1 2 3 4 5 6 8 9 10

- We or I know & understand the risk we're taking in all our savings/investments.
- I'm confident my investments match my retirement goals/objectives.
- I could weather a major market correction like 2008
- I know my Risk number on a scale from 1-100.

Scan the code below to listen to Don's recap

MEDICAL & LONG-TERM CARE CONTINGENCY PLANNING

What To Do With Life's Curve Balls That Can Ruin Your Retirement Plan

"Odds...They mean nothing until they work against you."

The "M" in ARMOR. Medical & Long-Term Care and Contingency Planning

LONG-TERM CARE - A 50% CHANCE

It's estimated that a married couple aged 65 or older has more than a 50% chance that one of them will need some form of long-term care. This is one of the greatest threats to your ARMOR UP income plan.

From my conversations with retirement-minded individuals, the rising cost of long-term care is a top concern. Long-term care expenses could be "the hole in the bucket," potentially draining your savings. Do you have a plan to handle a potential $7,000 monthly expense?

Common Assumptions About Long-Term Care

Many pre-retirees assume that Medicare will cover their long-term care needs. This is like assuming your auto insurance will pay for a new car if your house burns down.

Medicare is designed to cover specific services like skilled care, not custodial care—the ongoing living assistance most people require. Medicaid, on the other hand, is for those without financial resources to pay for care. As I often say, Medicaid has a "deductible," which is your net worth. To qualify, you must have virtually no money. Most people don't want to be in the financial position required to qualify for Medicaid.

A Case Study

Take Joe and Carol from our previous chapter. Let's say Carol has a debilitating stroke, and Joe is unable to care for her at home. Initially, Joe might try to be her primary caregiver, but this can take an emotional, physical, and psychological toll. Overwhelmed caregivers often become patients themselves.

Joe would need to find the best care for Carol, whether it's rehabilitation or a permanent facility. After Medicare and insurance cover their share, Joe could face monthly bills of $7,000 to $10,000. Where does that money come from? Their savings.

Personal Experience

I know this struggle personally. My father cared for my mother during her 16-year battle with Alzheimer's, assisted by professional aides. Watching his health decline under the strain of caregiving was heartbreaking. Ultimately, moving my mother to a memory care facility was the best decision for both of them, even though it was incredibly difficult for my dad. Without that choice, he may not have been able to care for her as long as he did—or even survive himself.

Mom and Dad

The Role of Long-Term Care Insurance

While ARMOR UP protects income for existing lifestyle and expenses, unexpected costs like long-term care require additional planning. A long-term care (LTC) insurance policy could help. For example, an LTC policy might pay up to $5,000 per month, leaving Joe to cover the remaining $2,000 from savings.

Many people dismiss the need for LTC insurance, assuming they'll never require care or that family will step in. But relying on "hope" is not a strategy. Odds mean little when you become part of the statistic.

Common Justifications Against LTC Insurance

Some reasons people give for not purchasing LTC insurance include:

- "I'll never need long-term care."
- "My parents didn't live long enough to need it."
- "My spouse will take care of me."
- "I'll just rely on my kids."

These assumptions often fail to consider the real burden placed on caregivers. Spouses or children may not be in a position to provide the level of care required, especially over the long term.

Alternative Care Options

If full-time care becomes necessary, facilities like adult day care centers or in-home care services can be great alternatives. For example, Visiting Angels, a franchise I purchased in 2002, offers non-skilled in-home care at half the cost of a visiting nurse. Many LTC policies cover such services, allowing individuals to remain in their homes longer and possibly avoid nursing homes altogether.

Questions to Ask Yourself

When planning for long-term care, consider these questions:

- Do I want to place this burden on my spouse or children?
- What happens if my spouse also needs care?
- Will relying on family actually save money?
- Are they truly in a position to help me?

Long-term care is expensive. Without a plan, it could quickly deplete your savings and leave your spouse in a precarious financial situation.

Moving Forward

The good news is that solutions exist to address long-term care expenses and ARMOR UP your savings. Let's discuss how we can create a strategy to protect your assets and provide peace of mind.

ARMOR UP OPTION 1: LONG-TERM CARE INSURANCE

Many people don't include long-term care insurance in their retirement budget. This is one of the main reasons many retirees don't have it, despite billions being paid out annually from these policies.

Let's revisit Joe and his wife, Carol. Recall their financial situation and how we used the ARMOR UP strategy to secure their income? It's an important reminder of why planning for long-term care costs is essential.

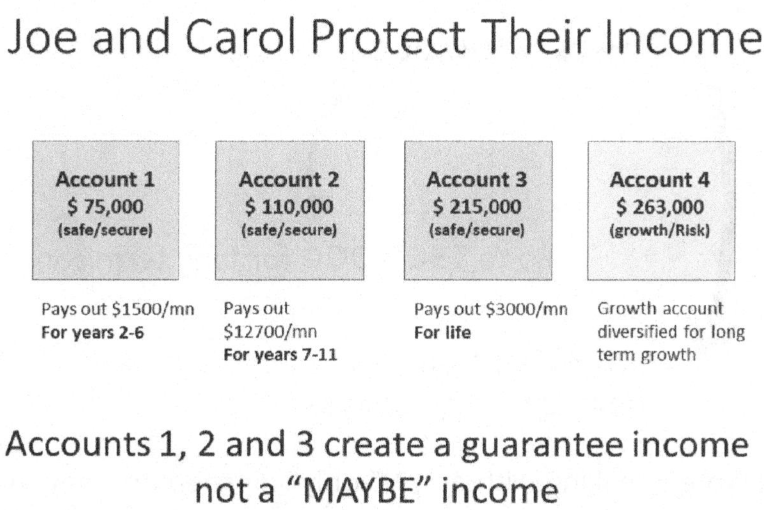

We have them direct 1½ percent of their Bucket #4 interest to create that ARMOR UP concept, creating protection between them and spend down.

Joe and Carol are not paying for this protection from their monthly budget. They are simply taking a little of their interest income.

ARMOR UP OPTION 2: ASSET-BASED PROTECTION

This option is an excellent strategy if you can use a lump sum or, for IRS purposes, make five annual deposits. Many people, like Joe and Carol, are in a position to make such a deposit. Imagine if their investment accounts were three or four times larger? Remember, their monthly expenses are already covered by our ARMOR UP income plan.

This approach involves a life insurance plan with a long-term care (LTC) component. For example, if Joe and Carol had an extra $200,000 sitting in CDs or a similar low-yield account, they could take half of that amount and use it for an asset-based plan with a one-time deposit.

Here is what that scenario could look like:

A DIFFERENT LONG TERM CARE SOLUTION

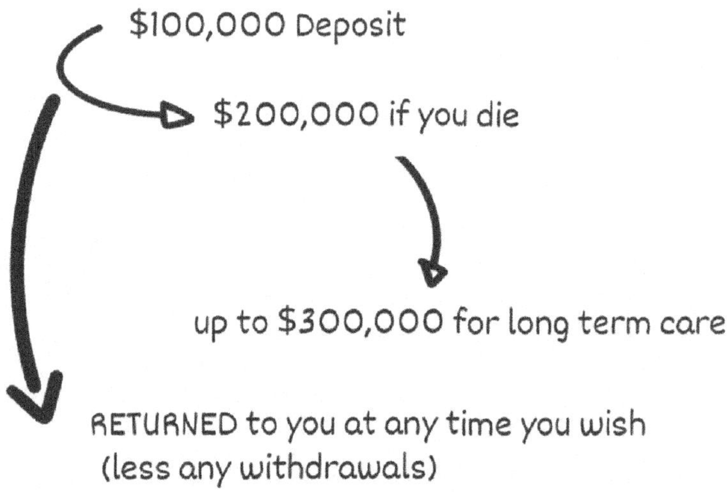

If you were speaking with an LTC-only salesperson, they might focus solely on traditional LTC insurance (Option 1). Why? Because they're only paid to sell that option. However, for those who can make a lump sum deposit like this, asset-based protection offers a powerful way to ARMOR UP your estate.

I know this is a high-level overview, but I'd be happy to meet with you and go over the details tailored to your specific situation.

ARMOR UP OPTION 3: DO NOTHING

This option falls under the category of the "hope" strategy. If we have the chance to meet—especially for readers who are not yet my clients—I'd like to discuss your hope strategy.

Let me clarify: there are individuals with significant high net worth who may not need to take any action. They could sell assets to cover almost any long-term care expense. What qualifies as high net worth? That depends on the situation, but for some, long-term care insurance may not be necessary.

That said, many high-net-worth individuals still choose to pursue coverage with Option 1 or Option 2. Why? Because it simply makes good financial sense.

OUR TEAM OF EXPERTS

At Ross Wealth Advisors, our philosophy for creating an abundant retirement is centered on designing a complete financial plan for our clients. Beyond that, we provide comprehensive support to address every aspect of retirement. We believe retirement planning goes far beyond just investment management. It requires a holistic approach, considering all facets of life after work.

To meet these needs, we've carefully selected a team of ancillary support experts who assist in areas like tax preparation, Social Security, Medicare, healthcare, insurance, real estate, estate planning, and even pre-planning a funeral. If you need an introduction to any of these resources, it is our pleasure to assist.

One of my favorite client stories involves a new widow, whom I'll call Elizabeth. During her most recent review meeting, she shared this with me:

"Don, I only have one telephone number I remember: 614-545-0277—Ross Wealth Advisors. Thanks to you, I know my money is safe, my estate plan is in good order, my taxes are done properly, and if I need anything else, I just give you a call."

Elizabeth now enjoys her winters in Florida and visits from her grandkids during spring break—all with peace of mind.

Speaking of family and loved ones, our next chapter will cover the critical topic of what happens when you pass away and how your assets are distributed. Planning for this stage is just as important as planning for your retirement itself. It's about protecting your legacy and ensuring your wishes are honored, whether it's gifting to heirs, churches, or charities. With the right strategies, we can even incorporate tax planning to maximize what you leave behind, potentially allowing you to give more than if you hadn't planned at all.

YOUR CHANCE TO EVALUATE YOURSELF

Rate your level of concern by circling 1-10. A rank of 1-6 indicates you have a level of concern. An 8, 9 or 10 means you have no concern.

Scan the code below to listen to Don's recap

Medical *Long-term Healthcare Plan* 1 2 3 4 5 6 8 9 10

- We or I have a plan to cover and pay for all my/our medical and healthcare needs
- I know my best options for all the various Medicare & supplemental coverage plans and I have a plan for paying nursing home care.

OUTSTANDING TAXES
Understanding Taxes In Retirement Accounts

"Just stop thinking of it as your money, and this will go a lot easier for the both of us."

Your Retirement Savings...Avoid this Tax "time" Bomb.

The "O" in ARMOR. Outstanding Taxes

UNDERSTANDING RETIREMENT ACCOUNTS: THE SHIFT FROM PENSIONS TO PERSONAL RESPONSIBILITY

In this chapter, I want to address some of the most common concerns and experiences shared by clients and prospective clients. Many investors are unaware of the intricacies and potential pitfalls that exist within retirement accounts. Let's explore these in greater detail.

What Are Retirement Accounts?

Retirement accounts encompass a variety of plans designed to allow participants to make tax-deductible contributions and benefit from tax-deferred growth. These include:

- **401(k) Plans**
- **457/Deferred Compensation Plans**
- **SEP IRAs**
- **Keogh Plans**
- **403(b)/Tax-Sheltered Annuities (TSAs)**
- **IRAs (Individual Retirement Accounts)**
- **DROP (Deferred Retirement Option Plans)** for Police and Firefighters

The Evolution of Retirement Accounts

Before the advent of 401(k) plans, most corporate and government retirement systems revolved around **defined-benefit pension plans**. These plans provided employees with a guaranteed income stream upon retirement, funded by their employers. Here's how they typically worked:

1. The employer contributed a portion of the worker's annual compensation to a pension fund.
2. 2Once fully funded and vested, the pension was handed over to an insurance company to manage and distribute payouts.

While these pensions offered security for many, they came with significant challenges:

- Companies needed consistent sales and profits to sustain funding.
- Economic downturns often left pension plans underfunded, jeopardizing payouts.

- During mergers and acquisitions, companies could legally extract "excess" cash from overfunded pension plans, leaving them vulnerable during market downturns.

The Decline of Defined-Benefit Pensions

Defined-benefit pensions gained popularity during the postwar boom, offering employers a way to retain valuable employees. However, over time, these plans became increasingly unsustainable:

- The expense of long-term guarantees to a large pool of workers was immense.
- Companies needed to set aside significant sums annually to maintain funding.
- When financial struggles arose, companies often raided pension funds to stay afloat—a practice permitted by the government.

As these challenges grew, large employers sought alternatives. The solution came in the form of changes to the IRS code that introduced tax-exempt retirement savings plans like the **401(k)** and **IRA**.

The Shift to Employee Responsibility

When 401(k) plans emerged, employers enthusiastically promoted them as a modern alternative to traditional pensions. At first, many companies matched employee contributions, positioning the 401(k) as an attractive and equitable option. This period of employer contribution helped cement the 401(k)'s reputation as a positive development, even though it shifted responsibility from the employer to the employee.

Over time, however, employer matches became less common, and the burden of saving for retirement fell squarely on the shoulders of individual workers. Unlike defined-benefit pensions, where income was guaranteed, these new plans placed the responsibility of funding, investing, and managing retirement savings directly on employees.

Why This Matters

This shift from employer-managed pensions to employee-managed retirement accounts has created new challenges:

- Employees must now navigate complex investment decisions.
- Market fluctuations directly impact their savings and future income.
- Hidden fees, tax implications, and contribution limits can erode returns if not properly managed.

Understanding the history and structure of retirement accounts is critical to making informed decisions about your financial future. As we delve deeper into this book, I'll share strategies to help you optimize your retirement savings and avoid common pitfalls.

HOW INVESTING YOUR RETIREMENT IN SECURITIES HAS CHANGED

The landscape of retirement investing has undergone significant changes over the decades. Thirty years ago, we were in the midst of a bull market where the value of investments seemed to climb endlessly.

During the 1990s, some mutual funds achieved staggering annual growth rates of 30% to 40%. Investors who "only" earned 20% returns would actually complain about what they considered underperformance. This era of remarkable growth shifted investor behavior and attitudes.

At the time, there was little interest in safer, more stable options like CDs from banks or guaranteed income streams from insurance companies. The prevailing mindset was: **"The stock market is the only place to make money."**

The Rise of 401(k)s, IRAs, and Mutual Funds

The introduction of 401(k)s and IRAs gave a massive boost to the mutual fund industry. Employee retirement contributions needed a home, and mutual funds became the default choice.

This influx of money into 401(k)s and IRAs created a self-reinforcing cycle:

- **Massive inflows** of retirement dollars were directed into mutual funds.
- As more money flowed in, the stock market saw higher returns.
- These returns attracted even more investors, further fueling market growth.

The phrase **"inflows to mutual funds"** became a hallmark of the era, with money pouring into Wall Street at an unprecedented rate, month after month and year after year. This constant inflow pushed equity markets higher, creating an environment where returns seemed almost guaranteed.

Fast Forward to Today

Now, we face a different reality. With thousands of people retiring daily, the dynamic is shifting. Retirees are no longer contributing to these investment vehicles—they are withdrawing from them to fund their retirement lifestyles.

This massive outflow of funds has significant implications:

- **Reduced inflows** to mutual funds could impact market performance.
- A greater reliance on withdrawals by retirees could increase market volatility.
- The need for income stability has become more critical than ever.

As we look ahead to the next 15 years, consider this: where do you think these retirees are pulling their funds from to cover their living expenses?

Exactly—from the same securities that once benefited from decades of inflows. This shift highlights the importance of reevaluating investment strategies to ensure your retirement savings are prepared for this new phase of the market.

NOW THE BAD WITH THAT GOOD...

Starting at age 73 (and age 75 beginning in 2033), account holders are required to take **Required Minimum Distributions (RMDs)** from their IRA and 401(k) accounts, marking the point where taxes on these tax-deferred accounts can no longer be postponed.

For decades, you've been contributing pre-tax dollars to these accounts, allowing them to grow tax-free. However, retirement is when the IRS finally steps in. Once you begin taking withdrawals—whether as required distributions or voluntary ones—those funds are treated as taxable income. The IRS, having patiently waited for its share, ensures that taxes are applied to every dollar you withdraw.

Even if you don't need the money, the government mandates these distributions, and every cent is subject to income tax. Whether you take out your savings as a lump sum or in installments, you'll face taxation on the entire withdrawal.

Implications for Your Heirs

The tax burden doesn't stop with you. Under current laws, heirs who inherit an IRA are required to empty the account within **10 years** of the original account holder's passing. This rule can create a significant tax liability for your beneficiaries, as large withdrawals over a short timeframe often push them into higher tax brackets.

What This Means for Your Planning

RMDs are a reality for anyone with a tax-deferred retirement account, but careful planning can help minimize the impact. By proactively addressing the timing and strategy of your distributions, you can better manage your tax obligations and protect your legacy for future generations.

HIGHLIGHTS OF THE RULES ON IRA WITHDRAWALS

All IRA withdrawals are subject to **ordinary income tax**. If you withdraw funds before age 59½, you may face an additional **10% early distribution penalty**, unless you qualify for specific exemptions such as:

- Disability
- Buying your first home
- Certain medical expenses
- Paying higher-education costs

Once you reach age 73 (75 starting in 2033), you must begin taking **Required Minimum Distributions (RMDs)** from your IRA. The first RMD must be taken by April 1 of the year after you reach this age, and each subsequent RMD must follow annually. These distributions are calculated using a formula based on your life expectancy. If you fail to take the RMD, you could face a **25% penalty** on the amount not withdrawn.

The Impact on Heirs

When you pass away with funds still in your IRA, your beneficiaries will inherit the account but must pay taxes on withdrawals. Under current rules, they are required to fully withdraw and pay taxes on the account balance within **10 years**, which can create a significant tax burden. For high-income heirs, the taxes on these withdrawals can be substantial, leaving them with far less than the original inheritance value.

The Real Cost of Taxes

The taxes on your IRA withdrawals may represent the largest check you ever write. Without proper planning, the costs could be staggering—not only for you but for your heirs as well. Poorly managed IRA distributions and inheritance strategies could result in thousands of dollars lost to taxes and penalties.

A Real-World Example

Let's look at a common scenario:

Who: Sarah, a retired police officer with $500,000 saved in her retirement plan.

Heirs: Tim and Carol, her son and daughter, both in their mid-50s earning $110,000 and $120,000 annually.

Situation: Sarah passes away, leaving her IRA to Tim and Carol.

Outcome: Tim and Carol inherit the $500,000 but face a significant tax bill as they must withdraw the entire amount within 10 years.

Under previous rules, Tim and Carol could have spread the withdrawals over their lifetimes, potentially growing the account to several million dollars. However, without proper estate planning, Sarah's IRA became a costly inheritance.

The Growing Challenge

The retirement landscape is rapidly changing. With the passing of the WWII generation and the ongoing retirement of baby boomers, an estimated **10,000 people retire daily**, leading to unprecedented movement of wealth. Many retirees are making mistakes as they roll over, withdraw, convert, or liquidate their retirement accounts—often due to poor advice or lack of knowledge.

Avoiding Costly Mistakes

To avoid these pitfalls, it's crucial to seek qualified, experienced advice. A knowledgeable advisor can help you navigate:

- **Roth IRA conversions:** Potentially reduce your future tax burden.
- **Net Unrealized Appreciation (NUA):** A tax-saving strategy for those with company stock in their 401(k).

- **401(k) rollovers:** Avoid unnecessary penalties and maximize your options.

One example of NUA in action: A client with P&G stock in their 401(k) saved thousands in taxes by moving their stock out correctly. This complex process requires expertise, so it's essential to work with an advisor who has experience with NUA strategies.

The Key Questions

As you consider your retirement accounts, ask yourself:

- **Do I roll over, withdraw, convert, or leave it alone?**
- **What strategies can I use to minimize taxes and maximize my savings?**

These decisions can have enormous financial implications. The wrong move could cost you thousands in fees and penalties, while the right strategy could save you just as much—or more.

Smart Tax Strategies

While taxes on retirement accounts are unavoidable, they can be minimized with careful planning. Strategies such as Roth IRA conversions or tailored withdrawal plans can significantly reduce the tax burden on you, your spouse, and your heirs.

The Bottom Line

The shift from employer pensions to personal retirement accounts gave savers more control but also more responsibility. Now that it's time to access these funds, the tax implications can be overwhelming. However, with the right knowledge and strategies, you can protect your wealth and minimize the impact of taxes.

Remember: **It's not about how much you make; it's about how much you keep.**

USING TAX LAWS TO YOUR ADVANTAGE

The following funny story illustrates using the rules to your advantage. It's about a rich man who lives in New York on the famous Island of Manhattan. The rich man is about to take a two-week trip, but before leaving he visits the bank to borrow $5,000 for the trip.

Here is the dialogue in that bank:

Rich Man: "Hello, Mr. Banker. I need to borrow $5,000 for two weeks."

Banker: "Sure, what do you have as collateral?"

Rich Man: "I own the Rolls Royce parked right out front."

Banker: "Sounds good to me. Here is your $5,000, see you in two weeks."

Banker Manager to Banker: "Please take that car and park it in a safe and secure place. I don't want a scratch on it."

Banker: "Yes sir. Done."

Two weeks later, Rich Man returns.

Banker: "Welcome back, Rich Man."

Rich Man: "Hello, here is the $5,000 I borrowed and the $68 of interest I owe you."

Banker: "Hold on Sir. I did some research while you were gone, and I discovered you are worth $20 million dollars. Why did you need a $5,000 loan for two weeks?"

Rich Man: "Where, young man, could I park a Rolls Royce in Manhattan for two weeks for $68 bucks?"

What is the point of this story? The Rich Man used the system, and laws to his advantage. I want to show you how to use the laws to your advantage. That's right. Let's put the rules and regulations to work for you. Remember, ARMOR UP your retirement savings accounts means saving you, your spouse, and your heirs from excessive fees and taxes.

FINAL THOUGHTS REMEMBER YOUR IRA IS AN IOU TO THE IRS.

One crucial point to keep in mind: your IRA represents a future tax bill. While these accounts have allowed you to save on taxes during your working years, withdrawals in retirement—and distributions left to heirs—are subject to taxation.

With current tax rates (2018–2026) at historic lows, now may be the ideal time to explore tax-free conversion strategies. By acting within this window, you could potentially save thousands of dollars in taxes over the course of your retirement.

Tax-Free Conversion Strategies

At Ross Wealth Advisors, we focus on three primary strategies for tax-free income:

1. **Roth IRAs**
2. **Municipal Bonds**
3. **LIRPs (Life Insurance Retirement Plans)**

Each of these options comes with its own set of advantages and considerations, which we align to your unique financial situation. If a tax-free strategy is a good fit for you, we'll have a detailed discussion to assess the best path forward.

Additionally, I have educational resources available, including another book, to help you understand these strategies in greater depth. If you're interested, let's discuss how we can position your retirement assets for long-term tax efficiency and peace of mind.

YOUR CHANCE TO EVALUATE YOURSELF

Rate your level of concern by circling 1-10. A rank of 1-6 indicates you have a level of concern. An 8, 9 or 10 means you have no concern.

Outstanding Taxes *Strategic Tax Plan* 1 2 3 4 5 6 8 9 10

- We or I have at least 2-4 tax strategies in place to reduce taxes for life.
- We or our current advisor have a comprehensive plan to permanently minimize or eliminate income taxes every year for the rest of our lives in retirement.
- Our estate plan minimizes the taxes my heirs will have to pay on their inherited assets.

Scan the code below to listen to Don's recap

RETIREMENT INCOME PLAN

FIXED INDEXED ANNUITIES (FIAS)

Our Bond Alternative Understand Them And Prosper

"It's not what you make on your money...it's what you keep."

—DON ROSS

The final "R" in ARMOR. Retirement Income Plan- Fixed Indexed Annuities (FIAs) and ARMOR UP your Cash Flow

Fixed Indexed Annuities (FIAs) are a safe-money and cash-flow product that may not be for everyone, but they are growing in popularity, making them worth discussing.

The goal of **Index Annuities**, often used as a bond alternative, is to earn interest linked to stock market gains with no risk to principal. The newer **Hybrid Income Annuities** build on this concept by offering additional benefits, such as **guaranteed lifetime income** that may increase annually.

These annuities combine pension-like features with greater flexibility. You can control your money, start receiving payments when needed, and even turn income on or off at will. Some Hybrid Income Annuities also provide increasing income for life, making them an attractive option for retirement planning.

The Safety of Insurance Companies

It's worth noting that annuities, including hybrids, are issued by insurance companies, which are subject to strict capital reserve requirements—much higher than those for banks. However, not all hybrid annuities are equal. Education is key to finding the best option for your needs.

How Index Annuities Work

Index Annuities protect your money while linking gains to a stock index, such as the S&P 500. They often have caps or limits on potential upside, but the trade-off is **no loss of principal**, even in a down market.

One important feature to consider is how often the annuity locks in gains, a process called **ratcheting**.

- **Annual ratcheting** locks in gains every year the stock market rises, ensuring those increases are preserved.
- **Longer ratchet periods**, such as every two years, increase the risk of losing gains to market volatility.

Popular Crediting Methods

Index Annuities use various crediting methods to calculate returns. Two common ones are:

1. **Annual Point to Point:** Resets yearly and compounds but may underperform in strong up years due to cap rates.
2. **Monthly Point to Point:** Performs well in steady upward markets but can lose gains from one or two bad months.

Both methods are based on S&P returns but behave differently, which is why diversification across methods may be beneficial.

Final Thoughts

Index Annuities don't directly participate in equities, bonds, or indexes, making them a safe option for preserving principal while earning moderate returns. If you're considering an FIA, I can explain the best crediting methods and options to suit your goals.

Together we can explore how these annuities can generate **guaranteed, reliable income**, helping you avoid the uncertainty of "maybe" income in retirement.

THE INCOME RIDER

The Income Rider is a new feature that allows you to turn on lifetime income **without annuitizing** (often referred to as "annuicide"). This means you retain control of your savings. In traditional annuities, when you annuitized, you gave up control of your money in exchange for guaranteed regular income. If you passed away, the insurance company often kept the remaining balance, and payments stopped.

With modern Hybrid Income Annuities, you no longer lose control. You can start and stop income payments as needed. This flexibility allows you to preserve your principal and reduce taxes when income isn't required. Later, when you turn payments back on, they may even be higher depending on the annuity's features.

Key Features of the Income Rider

1. **Lifetime Coverage for Two People**
   You can extend your annuity's income to cover both you and your spouse. If you pass away, the payments can continue for your spouse's lifetime, which is especially valuable if a spousal pension stops.
2. **Customizable Payment Periods**
   Income payments can be directed to yourself, another individual, or even a charity for a set period, such as 20 years.

3. **Lump-Sum Withdrawals**
   Certain annuities allow you to take a large sum of money for emergencies or personal desires, like medical expenses, buying a car, or funding a family vacation. However, large withdrawals may reduce future income payments or terminate the rider entirely, so careful planning is essential.

How Payouts Are Determined

Income Rider payouts depend on a **growth factor** based on your age and income account value. These growth rates can range from **4% to 7% annually**, depending on the annuity and insurance company. This growth applies to your **Income Account Value (IAV)**, which is used to calculate your income payouts.

The IAV grows annually, even if the stock market declines, until you begin taking income. The longer you wait, the higher your income payouts will be. However, it's important to understand that the IAV is not the same as your Account Value—it's specifically for calculating income payouts.

Why Expert Guidance Matters

Selecting an annuity with the **highest contractually guaranteed payout** is essential for your best interest. A knowledgeable retirement income specialist can help you navigate the options, ensuring you maximize benefits and maintain control of your money.

With an Income Rider, you gain flexibility, security, and control—all key to a well-**ARMORed** retirement plan.

The Three Worlds

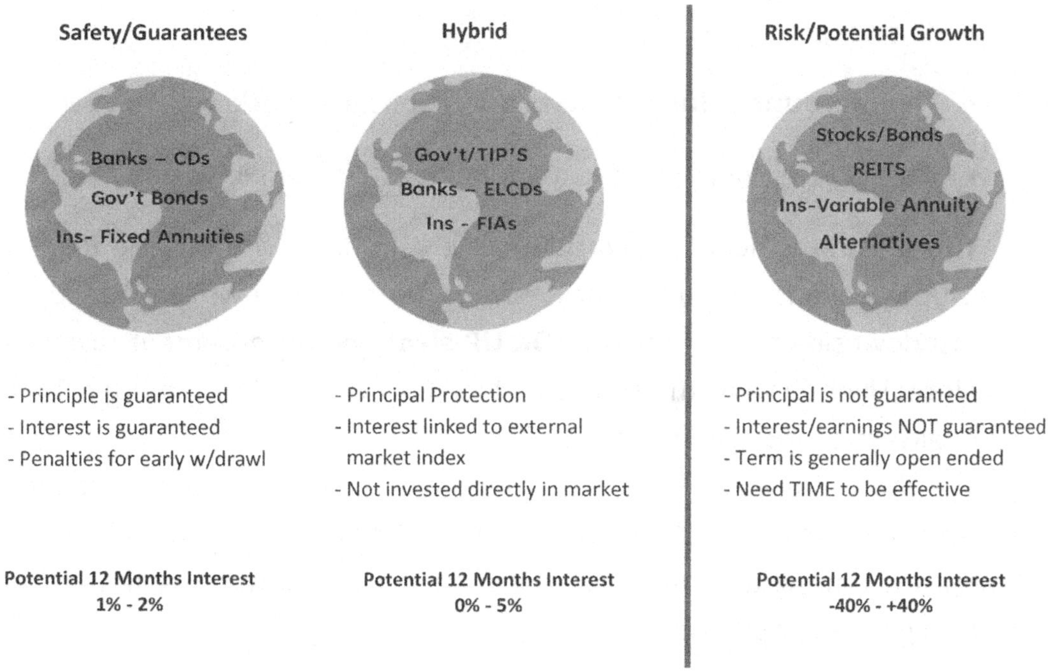

HYBRID

The **Hybrid** bucket in the Three Worlds chart shows where Hybrid/Index Annuities are positioned.

For those exposed to market volatility, a **Hybrid Income Annuity** provides guaranteed income. For example, if you invest $100,000 in a Hybrid Income Annuity at age 65, you could receive approximately $6,000 annually for life. This income could increase over time and may also provide benefits for a beneficiary or a joint payout with your spouse or another individual.

If you had invested the same $100,000 in mutual funds, you might have less today. Many mutual funds have underperformed the S&P 500 over the past decade. Relying solely on a strong stock market for an abundant retirement is risky.

By contrast, with a **Hybrid Income Annuity/FIA** with an Income Rider, your income account value would have significantly grown. This value, used to calculate your income, can grow at rates as high as 8% annually (depending on the company and interest rates).

Additionally:

- Your **account value** increases during positive stock market years.
- It stays level (with no losses) during negative market years.

This illustrates how FIA/Hybrid Income Annuities with Income Riders offer upside gains linked to stock market performance while protecting against downside risk—a key **ARMOR UP strategy** for retirement savings.

Note: Hybrid is a term used describing FIAs with an income rider. This is not always an Industry term.

The chart referenced compares the growth of your account value and income account value to the S&P 500 from 2000–2010. With millions of Americans retiring and ongoing market volatility, products like these are likely to grow in popularity.

Fixed Index Annuity The Power of Index Interest Crediting & Downside Protection

BENEFITS OF INDEX ANNUITIES WITH ANNUAL RESET

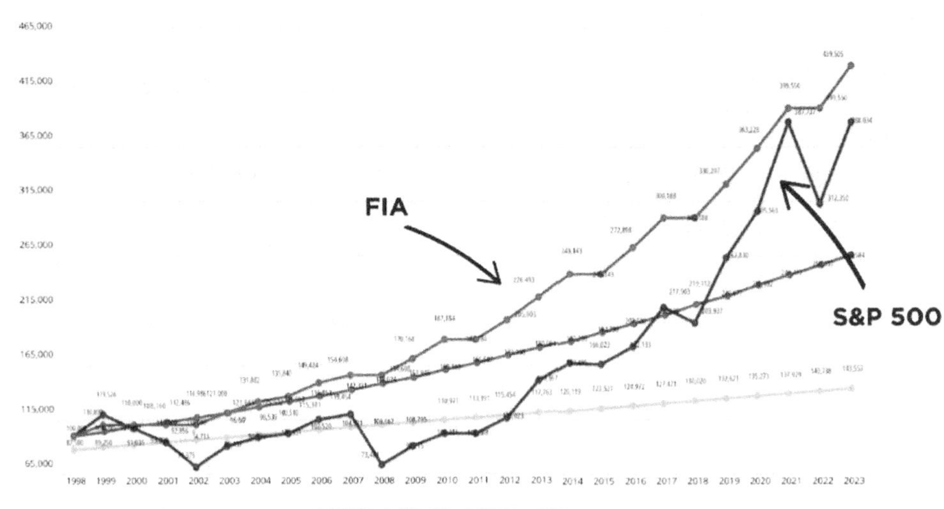

Above is a hypothetical comparison of the following: 1. Red line represents a $100,000 investment in the stock market that tracks the performance of the S&P 500 Index, excluding dividends. 2. Green line represents the $100,000 used to purchase a fixed index annuity with a x 10% cap rate index interest crediting method – based on the performance of the S&P 500 Index – with an interest rate floor of 0%. 3. Blue line represents the $100,000 initi premium compounding at a fixed interest rate of 4% per year. 4. Yellow line represents the contract's Minimum Guaranteed Surrender Value (MGSV), which is equal to 87.5% of the initial premium accumulated at an interest rate 1.00%. Any references to guarantees or lifetime income generally refer to fixed insurance products, never securities or investment products.

CONFINEMENT BENEFIT

A valuable feature of Hybrid Income Annuities (FIAs) is the **confinement benefit**, which doubles your income if certain conditions are met. For example, if a 75-year-old activates her guaranteed annual income of $10,603, it could double to $21,207 if she becomes confined (unable to perform specific daily activities).

The doubling of income is triggered based on the inability to perform **Activities of Daily Living (ADLs)**. Each annuity policy outlines the qualifying ADLs, but common examples include:

- Bathing
- Eating
- Dressing
- Walking
- Taking medications
- Getting out of bed or chairs

Most policies don't require you to be unable to perform all ADLs. Typically, being unable to perform two or three qualifies you for the increased income.

Insurance companies often advertise aggressively, hoping to be the first and only provider you consider when purchasing an annuity. They may send an agent to sell you their product quickly, discouraging comparison shopping. Avoid this mistake. Instead, work with an **independent fiduciary advisor** who can evaluate proposals from the highest-rated annuity providers to find the best fit for your needs.

One of the key strategies I implement for clients is finding the best combination of **safe-money products** to maximize income while minimizing the savings required. This ensures you get the highest possible income for the smallest investment, helping you preserve your assets while enjoying a secure retirement. That's an essential part of an **ARMOR UP plan**.

WHAT DOES EXTRA INCOME MEAN TO YOU?

Extra income in retirement can unlock a world of possibilities. It can fund vacations, dining at exceptional restaurants, or enjoying a truly abundant retirement. You could use it to diversify your portfolio, buy a new car, renovate your home, support your children or grandchildren, help relatives or friends, or donate to your favorite charities. That's the essence of a **retirement of abundance**.

Looking ahead, I believe products like Hybrid Income Annuities/FIAs will grow in popularity. Why? **Traditional pensions and company benefits are being cut back**, and governments are scaling back as well. The reality is that there's only so much money to go around, and the demands for those funds keep increasing.

The bottom line is that states, counties, cities, and corporations are struggling to afford the pensions they once promised. Even government employee unions are acknowledging this, agreeing to reforms that reduce pension contributions and payouts. Unfortunately, many corporate employees didn't take action to address shortfalls when their pensions were replaced with non-guaranteed 401(k) programs, leaving them to suffer the consequences.

I want to ensure the same doesn't happen to the millions of government workers still relying on their pensions. Today, many pensions are offering **partial or full lump-sum distributions**, which can be a significant benefit for those who act on the opportunity.

As governments and corporations face mounting deficits, layoffs have become more common. For example, in 2010, tens of thousands of government employees lost their jobs. Many workers now face the choice of accepting reduced pensions or risking further layoffs. Pension experts and union leaders agree that further reductions are inevitable, a topic now frequently covered in the media.

Yet, many financial advisors fail to recognize this **mega-trend**, leaving their clients unprepared for potential pension reductions. I see more government and corporate employees turning to us for retirement planning, seeking ways to make up for shortfalls in their pensions or 401(k) plans.

With new, safe, and innovative retirement solutions like Hybrid Income Annuities/FIAs, retirement-minded individuals can build plans that not only cover pension shortfalls but also significantly enhance their retirement income.

No matter what happens with your government pension or company-sponsored retirement plan, I can help you create a strategy for **retirement security**—one that's guaranteed to protect you from the actions of employers, politicians, inflation, the economy, or Wall Street. It's about crafting a **retirement of abundance** through an **ARMOR UP strategy**.

ARMOR UP YOUR CASH FLOW

"Retirement Income… It's About Cash Flow"

"I'm more interested in the return of my principal then I am return on my principal."
—WILL ROGERS

Retirement income planning is a specialty, and without proper care, financial mistakes can sneak up on you like an alligator. Let me share a lighthearted story to illustrate this point.

A wealthy man hosted a brunch for his friends and secretly had a truck-load of alligators placed in his pool. After brunch, he announced, "Whoever swims across the pool unharmed can have either my daughter's hand in marriage or half my wealth."

Suddenly, there was a loud splash, and one guest swam frantically to the other side, barely making it out alive. The man said, "That was amazing! Obviously, you want my daughter's hand in marriage." The swimmer replied, "No, Sir."

The man said, "Then you must want half my wealth." The swimmer again replied, "No, Sir." Perplexed, the man asked, "Then what do you want?" The swimmer said, "I want to know who pushed me into the pool!" The moral? Financial "alligators" exist, and you must avoid them.

At Ross Wealth Advisors, my goal is to help you **grow, enjoy, and protect your money** while reducing risks like inflation, volatility, taxes, and unplanned healthcare costs—all without additional out-of-pocket expenses. This is how we ensure your retirement is abundant.

In the Army, we studied our enemy to understand their strengths and strategies. In retirement planning, our "enemies" are **inflation, volatility, excessive taxes, inappropriate investing and unexpected illnesses**—all of which can erode your cash flow.

Inflation: A Hidden Threat

Do you remember gas prices in 1974? They were 26 cents a gallon, and attendants would pump your gas, check your fluids, and clean your windshield. Today, if two attendants approach your car, you'd lock the doors!

Inflation directly impacts retirees. What if Social Security cost-of-living adjustments stop? What if your pension is reduced? To combat inflation, you need a comprehensive strategy.

A simple way to estimate future inflation is with the **Rule of 72**:

- Divide 72 by the inflation rate to determine how many years it takes for prices to double.
    - At 4% inflation: prices double in 18 years.
    - At 3% inflation: prices double in 24 years.

Volatility: A Risk to Income

Some financial advisors suggest withdrawing 4% annually from your portfolio, but this can fail due to market fluctuations. For consistent, reliable income, you must use safe money vehicles properly structured for **cash flow**.

Wall Street may promise average returns of 10%, but how many people actually achieve that consistently? Few, and those who do often take on more risk than is advisable for retirement savings.

Avoiding the "Financial Junk Drawer"

Many pre-retirees and retirees have a "financial junk drawer"—a collection of products and investments without a cohesive strategy. High returns aren't always the solution; they often come with high risk, which hurt many people during the 2000-2001 and 2008-2009 market crashes.

For guaranteed, reliable monthly income, focus on **safe money vehicles** for cash flow, leaving higher-risk investments for growth accounts. Structuring your retirement savings to combat inflation and volatility requires a specialist who understands how to fit all the pieces together for an abundant and secure retirement.

Don't let financial "alligators" sneak up on you. Let's ARMOR UP your retirement savings and secure your financial future.

To wrap up the point; the right tools must be used to structure your retirement income properly. To do so, separate your retirement savings into two categories:

1. Safe money that provides you cash flow
2. At risk money that provides long-term growth

THE FINANCIAL PYRAMID

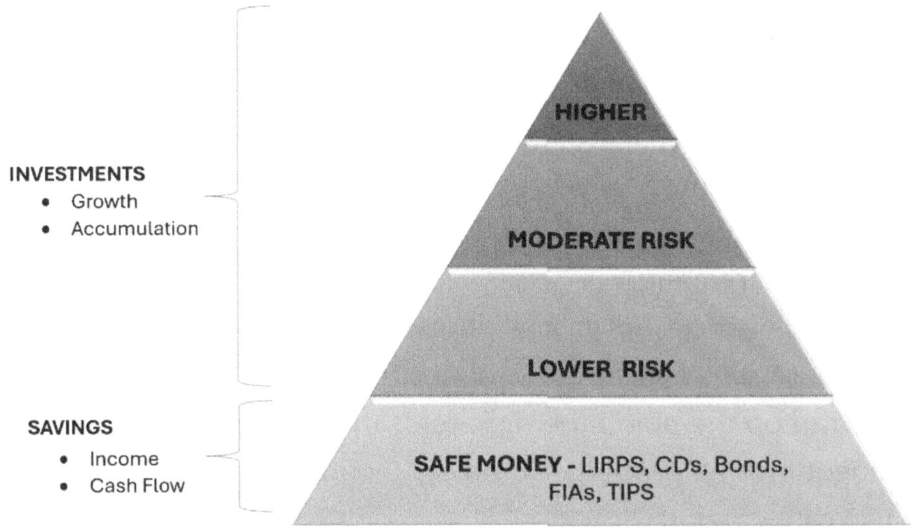

This chart drives home the point of safe versus at risk money. For income and The chart above highlights the difference between **safe money** and **at-risk money**. For **income and cash flow**, we rely on **savings vehicles**. For **growth and accumulation**, we use **risk vehicles** like investments.

The **DR Rule of 100** is illustrated here as well. It shows how a 70-year-old retiree's money might be allocated:

- **70% safe money**, structured for lifetime income using properly designed safe vehicles.

- **30% growth money**, allocated for long-term growth and inflation protection.

Safe money includes instruments that provide guarantees, such as **CDs, TIPS, Income Annuities (FIAs)**, and **government bonds and other alternatives**; investments not correlated to the stock market.

ARMOR UP: Protecting Your Retirement

Once we've identified the threats to your retirement (like inflation) and the tools to provide safe money, it's time to **structure your income for the long haul** using the **ARMOR UP strategy**.

ARMOR UP means protecting your retirement savings to ensure your income is reliable, ongoing, and safeguarded against inflation. While growth or "at-risk" money combats inflation in a properly structured stock/bond portfolio, it can later transition to safe money when additional income is needed.

Think of ARMOR UP like putting on body armor—it shields your income savings while providing peace of mind.

Now, let's focus on income. Imagine we're meeting in my office, and I'm helping you ARMOR UP your savings. After considering your pension (if applicable) and Social Security, there's still a shortfall of $2,500 per month.

Case Study: Joe and Carol

- **Joe:** Age 65, retired
- **Carol:** Age 63, retired
- **Joe's Pension:** $73,500 per year ($6,125 per month)
- **Monthly Expenses:** $7,550
- **Monthly Shortfall:** $1,425 today, projected to increase to approximately $2,000 in 10 years and $2,900 in 20 years
- **Savings:** $673,500 (IRAs and non-IRAs)

When Joe and Carol came to me, their savings had been nearly $900,000 before the 2008 market crash. To fill their income gap, we must make the most efficient use of their remaining $673,500 by incorporating **Safe Vehicles**.

ARMOR UP STRATEGY

The ARMOR UP plan will use "Buckets" to allocate funds, ensuring reliable income regardless of stock market or economic conditions. The priority is to generate consistent income, as Joe and Carol depend on this money for their retirement security.

By focusing on a strategy that minimizes risk and maximizes efficiency, we can protect their savings while addressing their income needs. This approach ensures peace of mind and financial stability throughout their retirement years.

Note: For illustration purposes, all numbers are net. Of course, we calculate taxes and inflation.

Joe and Carol Protect Their Income

Account 1 **$ 75,000** **(safe/secure)**	**Account 2** **$ 110,000** **(safe/secure)**	**Account 3** **$ 215,000** **(safe/secure)**	**Account 4** **$ 263,000** **(growth/Risk)**
Pays out $1500/mn **For years 2-6**	Pays out $12700/mn **For years 7-11**	Pays out $3000/mn **For life**	Growth account diversified for long term growth

Accounts 1, 2 and 3 create a guarantee income not a "MAYBE" income

ARMOR UP YOUR RETIREMENT SAVINGS

The chart above illustrates how we apply the **ARMOR UP strategy** using Buckets. Let me guide you through it step by step. Keep in mind, this is just one example. Your solution will be tailored to your unique goals and circumstances, as every client's plan is customized to fit their needs.

- **Safe money** is in Buckets One, Two, and Three.
- **Risk money** for long-term growth is in Bucket Four.

In this example, Bucket One begins paying Joe and Carol in the second year, as they had enough cash to cover their expenses in the first year. Bucket One then pays out from years two through six.

- **Bucket Two:** Pays from years seven to twelve.
- **Bucket Three:** Provides lifetime income starting in year twelve.

These buckets cover the shortfall in their monthly expenses and give Joe and Carol peace of mind. They no longer have to worry about the economy, stock market performance, or outliving their money. If Joe passes before Carol or vice versa, or even if they both pass away at the same time, any remaining funds in the buckets go to their heirs. That's the abundance they wanted.

Bucket Four

The $263,000 not used in the first three buckets is invested in a **diversified, disciplined portfolio** for long-term growth. Since these funds are not needed for monthly expenses, market fluctuations are acceptable. Bucket Four hedges against inflation, so if 15 years down the road the $3,000 per month from Bucket Three isn't enough, these funds can supplement their income.

By adjusting for inflation, income increases over time, and we can modify the plan annually if needed.

Why This Strategy Works

The **ARMOR UP strategy** fit Joe and Carol perfectly. Here's why:

- If they live 20 years, they would have withdrawn at least $464,000, with Bucket Three still providing lifetime income.
- Bucket Four, earning 5% annually, could grow to approximately $856,000.

They started with $673,000, enjoyed $464,000, still have guaranteed income, and maintain an investment account valued at $800,000 or more. That's the power of **ARMOR UP!**

Common Challenges with Other Advisors

Many advisors focus only on **accumulation**—growing money—but lack the expertise to create income-focused plans. Taking monthly income from a volatile account is risky, yet it's a common practice.

Three out of five new clients at Ross Wealth Advisors come from existing advisor relationships. Often, these clients realize their previous advisors didn't provide solutions for **retirement income, tax reduction, healthcare, or estate planning**. After seeing our approach, they recognize the difference and appreciate our specialization in retirement planning.

Worry-Free Retirement

Retirement should be a **worry-free zone**. You've worked hard to save, and money should not be a source of stress. There are plenty of other concerns—adult children, grandchildren, health—but income doesn't need to be one of them.

However, I strongly advise against trying to ARMOR UP your funds on your own. The products and strategies used in this plan are complex, like pieces of a puzzle. It takes a specialist to design a cohesive, strong plan that ensures your financial peace of mind.

SOCIAL SECURITY

Social Security is a complex program that can be challenging to navigate. There are numerous options for couples and individuals when determining benefits, and decisions should be tailored to your unique situation. While it's helpful to hear what friends and neighbors are doing, I encourage you to take advantage of a powerful tool we use that maps out the most optimal time for you to access your benefits.

Although this book does not dive deeply into Social Security, it remains a vital component of our overall retirement planning strategy.

YOUR CHANCE TO EVALUATE YOURSELF

Rate your level of concern by circling 1-10. A rank of 1-6 indicates you have a level of concern. An 8, 9 or 10 means you have no concern.

Retirement Income Plan	1	2	3	4	5	6	8	9	10

- We or I have a written, yearly income plan detailing which accounts including Social Security and pensions, to draw from and when.
- I know how all our assets and income will be taxed when we receive, sell, or take withdrawals from them.
- I'm confident our money will last for my/our lifetime.

Scan the code below to listen to Don's recap

CONCLUSION

BUILDING A PLAN TOGETHER

When seeking financial advice for retirement, you need a specialist trained in retirement planning strategies. After age 50, the time to recover from mistakes is shorter. A well-diversified plan is essential not just for enjoying the retirement you've dreamed of but also for the peace of mind to live it fully.

You've likely been saving for retirement in the same way for years, and change might feel uncomfortable. However, transitioning from accumulation to preservation and income often requires it. A small mistake could mean the difference between independence or moving in with your adult children later.

I prefer in-person visits when possible, as building a personal relationship helps us better understand and exceed your expectations. At Ross Wealth Advisors, we consider our clients part of the family, and your concerns, dreams, and goals matter deeply.

Think of this analogy: If you need knee replacement surgery, would your family doctor perform it? Of course not. Like an accumulation advisor, they can only do so much. Now is the time to work with a specialist trained to guide retirement-minded individuals through comprehensive plans, including Investment Strategies, Income Planning, Legacy, Tax Reduction, and Long-Term Healthcare Planning.

When choosing a specialist, consider these questions:

- Do I trust this person?
- Do I like this person? (Very important)
- What does their planning process look like?
- Are they a fiduciary/independent advisor?
- Are they addressing my concerns?
- Are we connecting well?
- Are they objective and unbiased?
- Do they offer a team approach with other retirement resources?
- Are they moving at a pace comfortable for me?
- What do their fees look like?
- Did I research them via FINRA, the Better Business Bureau, or the National Ethics Bureau?
- Are we philosophically aligned?

The advisor relationship is a long-term partnership that can span decades. If you're reading this, you may not have worked with a financial advisor yet, or you may be questioning if your current advisor is right for this stage of your life. Many excellent "accumulation" advisors exist, but is that focus enough now?

I'd love the opportunity to meet with you and explore how we can work together.

A FEW FINAL THOUGHTS...

Thank you for taking the time to read this book. My goal is to provide you with valuable information to help you make informed decisions about what I consider one of the most exciting chapters of life—your retirement years.

As I always say, "An educated consumer is a winning consumer!" I'm genuinely interested in hearing the concerns of those who are retirement-minded. It's a two-way street—I enjoy educating others, but I also learn so much from the people I meet each day.

This is the best job, during the best times.

If we have the chance to meet, I can assure you our time together will be valuable. Your retirement goals will be the focus as we navigate Investment, Income, Legacy, Tax Reduction, and Healthcare planning.

Your concerns are important to me, and just as you will learn from our conversation, I know I'll learn something new from you as well.

Let's start building your abundant retirement today. ARMOR UP!

Sincerely,

Don Ross, RFC®

Registered Financial Consultant Retirement Income Planning Specialist
Member of The Council of Financial Educators

ARMOR UP SELF-EVALUATION

Please rate your level of concern in all 5 key areas for retirement. A rank of 1-6 indicates you have concern's (7's not allowed). An 8, 9 or 10 means you have no concern.

Estate Plan	1	2	3	4	5	6	8	9	10

- We or I know our assets will transfer according to our wishes when we're gone.
- We have a will and/or trust(s)/POA's in place and it's been updated within the last 3 years and it is properly funded.
- Our estate plan is coordinated with our retirement plan to maximize benefits and lower taxes.

Investment Plan	1	2	3	4	5	6	8	9	10

- I could weather a major market correction like 2008.
- I know my risk number on the 1-100 scale.
- We or I know & understand the risk we're taking in all our savings/ investments.
- I'm confident my investments match my retirement goals/objectives.

Income Plan 1 2 3 4 5 6 8 9 10

- We or I have a written, yearly income plan detailing which accounts including Social Security and pensions, to draw from and when.
- I know how all our assets and income will be taxed when we receive or take withdrawals from them.
- I'm confident our money will last for my/our lifetime.

Tax Reduction Plan 1 2 3 4 5 6 8 9 10

- We or I have at least 2-4 tax strategies in place to reduce taxes for life.
- We have a comprehensive plan to permanently minimize or eliminate income taxes every year for the rest of our lives.
- We have a plan to minimize RMDs and the taxes on these distributions.
- Our estate plan minimizes the taxes my heirs will have to pay on their inherited assets.

Long Term Healthcare 1 2 3 4 5 6 8 9 10

- We or I have a plan to cover and pay for all my/our medical and healthcare needs
- I know my best options for all the various Medicare & supplemental coverage plans and I have a plan for paying nursing or in-home care.

For further self-evaluation, visit our educational site www.833ARMORUP.com

Made in the USA
Monee, IL
14 September 2026

62974525R00063